CELIBACY
a love story

CELIBACY
a love story

Memoir of a Catholic Priest's Daughter

Mimi F. Bull

BAUHAN PUBLISHING ✦ PETERBOROUGH ✦ NEW HAMPSHIRE

2019

For my family

Library of Congress Cataloging-in-Publication Data
Names: Bull, Mimi, author.
Title: Celibacy, a love story : memoir of a Catholic priest's daughter / Mimi Bull.
Description: Peterborough : Bauhan Publishing, 2019.
Identifiers: LCCN 2019015898 | ISBN 9780872332867 (softcover : alk. paper)
Subjects: LCSH: Bull, Mimi. | Children of clergy—Biography. | Priests. | Catholic Church—Clergy.
Classification: LCC BX4705.B9824 A3 2019 | DDC 282.092 [B] —dc23
LC record available at https://lccn.loc.gov/2019015898

Book and cover design by Henry James
Cover Photographs: Mimi's mother, Florence Foyette *(left)* at Cape Cod Canal; Mimi's father, Fr. Hippolyte Zawalich *(right)*, ca. 1934; Mimi Foyette Bull *(center)*, at Craigville Beach, Cape Cod, age 8.

BAUHAN
PUBLISHING LLC
PO BOX 117 PETERBOROUGH NEW HAMPSHIRE 03458
WWW.BAUHANPUBLISHING.COM
603-567-4430

Follow us on Facebook and Twitter– @bauhanpub

MANUFACTURED IN THE UNITED STATES OF AMERICA

On one of his last days,
my husband struggled to his feet
and laid his hands on my shoulders,
securing my full attention. Long a witness to
my efforts to untangle the web of lies hiding
my identity, he gazed directly into my eyes
and spoke his final, hoarse words:

Speak Speak Speak!

PROLOGUE

A Letter to the Pope

"Your Holiness . . ."

T HOSE ARE THE WORDS I found myself calmly typing into my
laptop one afternoon in September 2017. How else to begin
such a letter? Many years of living abroad in the 1960s and early
1970s had turned me into a prolific correspondent. Before afford-
able phone calls, email, or Skype, letters were the only vital link
to my family and friends back in the States. My desk always held
a pile of mail to be answered, but writing to the Pope had never
been on my "to do" list. Now, most unexpectedly, it was.

A month earlier, I had learned that the special *Boston Globe* in-
vestigative team, called Spotlight, had published two long articles
about the children of Catholic priests. Fourteen years earlier, the
same team had produced a lengthy Pulitzer-winning exposé on
the shockingly extensive child abuse perpetrated over many years
by clergy in the Boston diocese, a story that became the basis for
the 2015 Oscar-winning film, *Spotlight*. After reading these latest
articles, I emailed the writer, Michael Rezendes, to inquire if he
knew of any group or individual whom I might contact to share
this experience, for, in all my eighty years, I had never knowingly
spoken with anyone who, like me, was the child of a practicing
Catholic priest. He responded by asking if he might interview
me for a follow-up article, and though I tentatively agreed, I had
misgivings. I had grown up in an era when you were supposed to

appear in the newspaper only at birth, marriage, and death; deeply ingrained "shoulds" and "should nots" loomed up in my thoughts. I would be exposing my parents' most heavily guarded secret, one that had hung over their adult lives like a Damoclean sword. Could I trust this man?

Rezendes (played in the film by Mark Ruffalo), being a member of the now-famous Spotlight team, was easy to research. The profiles and interviews that I discovered online were enough to get a sense of him and to assure me that he would treat my story with the care and sensitivity it deserved. My instincts, as it turned out, were well rewarded, and, as he rightly foretold, I have not regretted adding my account to the growing body of stories that a hitherto-silent congregation of children of priests is now stepping out of the shadows to relate.

The third *Globe* article appeared on October 1, 2017, hurried along by an announcement from the Vatican that it had finally agreed to establish policy and guidelines for bishops dealing with priests who had fathered children and to include these children in its Commission on the Welfare of Children. Nothing about this delicate issue had ever been covered in the Church's vast body of canon law that dictates the policy of its governance. After many centuries of a failed celibacy policy and the church hierarchy's resolute denial and neglect of the resulting children and their mothers, another large and particularly shameful skeleton was at last being driven out of the Vatican closet—and spot-lit.

Mike remembered that I had never spoken to another priest's child, and as he wrapped up our interview he suggested that I call Vincent Doyle, whom he had profiled in the Spotlight series on August 17, 2017. Vincent, a young Irish psychotherapist from Connemara and himself the son of a priest, had founded Coping International, an organization for children of priests. He had worked closely with members of the Irish Catholic hierarchy to create guidelines for bishops dealing with this problem, and then

traveled to Rome to put their policy amendment proposal directly into the hands of Pope Francis. Included in the proposal was a
challenge that a date be set in September 2017 for the convening
of a special commission to look into the Church's nearly millenni-
um-long avoidance of such a policy.

More eager to finally compare notes with another child of a
priest than to ponder Church policy or Vatican commissions, I
immediately dialed the number Mike had given me and was soon
swept up in the whirlwind of activity that is Vincent Doyle. It
was evening in Ireland when my call went through, and he was
relaxing in his thatched cottage near the Connemara coast with his
dogs and a coffee close by. His brogue carried me deep into good,
rich talk laced with humor as we shared our stories. His kindness,
compassion, and irresistible enthusiasm lured me into considering
his request, slipped in along the way, to write to the pope. "No
pressure, now, Mimi," he said. "I mean no disrespect." Because
I was the oldest child of a priest to emerge thus far, and because I
had lived and dealt with the full range of the experience, he felt I
might have a powerful voice on the subject. I frankly had no idea
what I might write in such a letter, but when the time came a few
weeks later, the letter wrote itself.

I wept after I hung up with Vincent. Our conversation trig-
gered a powerful and unexpected release, perhaps because it exposed, at last, a final layer of the metaphorical onion I had been
peeling for so many years. I had never before felt recognition and
affirmation from another priest's child, a person who shared with
me that bewildering experience and who therefore understood the
nuances and the singularity of our peculiar life's journey. And I
had never realized, until that moment, how deeply I had longed
for, and profoundly needed, such a fellow traveler.

It never occurred to me—until Vincent's timely and therapeu-
tic suggestion—that I might throw off the burden of my Catholic
training and, by directly addressing the Church, express at least

some of my deeply buried anger with the powerful institution whose long reach had begun shaping my life before I had even taken my first breath. The Church's harsh dictates had circumscribed a large portion of my world and inhibited so many of my actions within its often-suffocating circumference. How many times in the course of my life, for instance, had I found myself asking, *Who do I think I am to: invite this person to my home,* or *ask help from that person,* or *express my opinion in this group,* or even, most depressingly, *take up space...?*

At the most basic existential level, then, I needed to announce myself to a rigidly patriarchal institution that, in refusing to acknowledge my existence in any way, drew a veil over my true identity and, therefore, by extension, over my experience of the truth of that which primarily defines us as social beings: our ties to community, friends, and family.

Most damaging of all, it rendered me invisible to myself. One of my first unconscious responses to the complexity of my situation can be found in the name I innocently gave to my imaginary friend, to whom I talked endlessly during my early childhood.

I called her "Realgirl."

PART ONE

—What does your father do?

—I don't have a father.

—Why not?

—Because I was adopted by two women.

—Dear, the agencies don't give children to single women.

—Well, this was a special case!

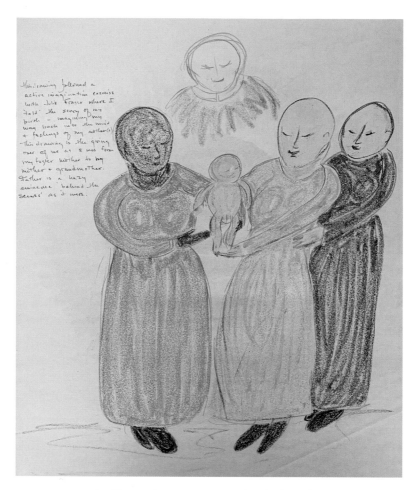

Art Therapy Drawing No. 1 – The Three Mothers

This is the first in a series of drawings that I made for a Lesley College class in Art Therapy in the spring of 1992. After an "active imagination" exercise in which I "told" the story of my birth, I drew the scene of being handed over, at age eight-and-a-half months, by my anonymous foster mother (in blue) to Alice (in green) and Florence (in red). Floating above them is Father Hip, a benign gray eminence.

EVEN THOUGH, GROWING UP, I didn't spend a lot of time thinking about my status as an adoptee, it was the back story to my childhood. I'd been told that I was adopted early on, and more information filtered down as I grew into adulthood: Alice Foyette adopted me in July of 1937 in Philadelphia when I was eight-and-a-half months old and brought me back to Norwood, Massachusetts, to live with her and her grown daughter, Florence. They had told me as soon as I was old enough to understand the concept of adoption that they had wanted a boy, but I seemed so much brighter than the little boy who was also available that they decided to adopt me instead. I loved that story and clung to that first glimmering of the value of talent. Adoption set me apart. I was the only adopted child I was aware of. If others were adopted, one didn't know because such things weren't discussed. In my case, however, as the child in a family of two women, my adopted status was necessarily known. It simply "was what it was" in my mind and that was that.

+ + +

My first inkling that I wasn't who I thought I was came years later in 1970, when I was thirty-four. Florence, whom I'd considered my adoptive mother since Alice's death in 1943, had come down to Princeton, New Jersey, where I had recently moved with my husband, Neil, and our three children. Since my childhood, I had been accustomed to having serious talks with my mother in the car while driving somewhere, anywhere. A few days into her visit, she asked if we might go off together for the afternoon.

Neil's work as a headmaster had taken us overseas and out West for long stints, yet my mother and I had remained closely connected by our frequent letters. I did not consider how my quite different life might begin to form an emotional barrier that she found increasingly difficult to cross. Nor did I think, in the midst of my own adjustment to our recent move, about how lonely the departure of her only child would make her. She had been a working mother with no spouse, parents, or siblings when I married Neil. My urge to justify her hard work on my behalf kept me from showing her anything less than happiness and success in my life. And she never asked me to share any difficulties I might be having—quite the contrary. Her own matriarchal Polish mother had ruled her life to such an extent that she'd resolved never to interfere in mine. My need to tell her a positive story was entirely self-imposed. I was convinced that I must not disappoint her with anything less than success. But something was in the air now; I could feel it when she suggested that we go out for a drive. Perhaps she needs to vent, I thought. But what she said came completely out of the blue and was far beyond the realm of my speculations. We were driving through the farmland that surrounded Princeton in those days when she turned to me and said, "Mimi, I want you to know that I am your real mother."

It blinded me as one is blinded by light after a blindfold is removed. At that moment of confusion, I could only grasp my supreme sense of happiness in knowing that this woman whom I so loved was indeed my real mother and not my adoptive sister/second adoptive mother, as I had been raised to believe. Out of blurred recollections of childhood, I remembered the day when I was six, shortly after Alice died, when Florence had suggested to me that now I should call her "Mummy." That had been as easy for me as putting on a new blouse. She had been my sister, always there and as dear to me as her mother, Alice, had been. Hearing me call her "Mummy" for the first time must have been for her a deeply charged experience.

An adopted child holds on to an odd set of impressions concerning her origins, and there is a sense of apartness that pervades her relationship to everything. Sometimes I took refuge in the fantasy that one is a special child sent to live in simple circumstances for training in life. I particularly loved the fairy tale of the Princess and the Pea, which resonated with me very deeply. I imagined myself on that day when, cold and lost, I would knock at the castle door and be welcomed and, most importantly, recognized for who I really was. I had spent a lot of time alone as a child, with the made-up Realgirl to share my games. Only many years later, after I had found all the pieces of my incomplete jigsaw puzzle childhood, did I grasp the irony of the name I gave my imaginary playmate.

I must have pulled the car to the side of the road and hugged my mother in utter relief and happiness. I have tried imagining what she felt that day. A proud and intelligent woman who lived with an intense level of shame and sacrificed her own dreams and aspirations in order to keep me as her own, she remains for me a fascinating mystery. I can only hope my elation was a satisfying reward and affirmation of her courage.

My mother had made her difficult disclosure and that was the end of the truth-telling. For when I posed the inevitable follow-up question, "What about my father?" she answered casually:

"Oh, he never knew about you. It was a brief encounter, I was innocent about sex, and I never saw him again."

"Who was he?"

"A business executive from Pennsylvania. I've forgotten the details."

She closed down and would say no more. No argument of mine regarding health history or family background for my children's sake, or the simple fact that I was an adult and mature enough to handle the truth—nothing weakened her resolve to keep me in the dark about my father. But also, I was too shaken and moved by the revelation that she had, herself, given birth to me, a revelation for which she had heroically prepared herself. I did not press her further.

My efforts would have proved fruitless anyway, on that or any other day, for she resisted divulging my father's identity (to me) right to her final breath. The topic was strictly off limits. She had grown up without her own father, whose marriage to her strong-willed mother was over when she was still an infant. And though she did not have the chance to develop a relationship with him, she at least knew his identity and knew his (and thus, her) family background. She did not seem to comprehend the importance to me of having this fundamental piece of information. As a result, she did not recognize my visceral need to know, and, uncharacteristically, she failed to empathize with my anguish of not knowing. It seemed that the shame and taboo around this point were just too powerful to be surmounted by any maternal concern for my well-being.

My husband was not surprised by Florence's confession. He said that the first time he'd met my mother and seen us together he knew the cover story was a charade—but figured that if that was the way we had chosen to play it, he would go along. I, on the other hand, had believed my mother's story of my adoption completely. There had never been any hint along the way that it was otherwise. Florence asked that we not tell my children, and I regret now that I honored her request. And so they went on assuming she was my adoptive mother and felt the same degree of distance from her as I had with my mother's family. They felt affection for her as a familiar and beloved figure in their world, but missed out on the feeling of subtle connection one has with one's flesh and blood. They told me this much later when all of that changed.

That afternoon's ride in the Delaware Valley began a fifteen-year period of rebuilding my life story and searching for its missing pieces. For, as I came to discover, not one detail of my background, the circumstances of my existence, my relation to the people in my childhood, nor, indeed, my sense of who we all were—none of it was true. By altering one crucial detail of my story with her pronouncement, my mother had changed everything.

In one respect, however, things remained the same. Florence had revealed the truth of our connection to me only; the secret still had to be kept from my aunts and cousins, as well as my own children. In the eyes of my family, I was still Florence's adopted daughter.

At some point during these fifteen years—a period of deep self-reevaluation, when so much was being torn down and re-built—I had a dream that gave me a radiant sense of optimism and well-being:

> I am a small child walking alone in a dark wood.
> I come to a large, sunlit clearing where there is a
> pool. I plunge in and from the bottom of the pool
> I scoop up what seem to be small colored pebbles.
> When I come back to the surface and inspect them
> in the sunlight, they prove to be a collection of
> carved pieces of jade, ivory, coral, and semi-pre-
> cious stones, along with gold.

The dream was so clear and singular that it made an indelible impression. It still gives me a frisson of pleasure when I recall it.

I should add that there was at least one notable instance, a decade earlier, when Florence tacitly declared, by means of an omission, the truth of her motherhood. When it came time to prepare for my wedding, it naturally fell to her, as mother of the bride, to oversee the printing and issuing of the announcement and invitations, a process that involved the etching of two copper plates, one for each mailing.

Copper plate used to print my
wedding announcement

The truth is there in the second line, in the words "her daughter." At the time, I did not dwell on the significance of that pairing; there was too much on my mind, and my mother and I were not in the habit of discussing this hot topic. Of course, she never consulted me about her decision to omit "adopted" between the words "her" and "daughter." I think that lie would have been too large, even for her,

Reverend Hippolyte Zawalich

to stomach at such an important transition in both of our lives—one that marked the culmination of all she had been working and sacrificing for since my birth. It would seem odd now, at a time when adoptive parents are seen as absolutely "real" parents, to add the word "adopted" to a wedding invitation. But that was the adjective that had always accompanied our relationship—and was required by her status at the time as an unmarried woman. She could not bring herself to publish the lie, and preferred instead to face the possibility of lifted eyebrows when the stiff cream envelopes were received and the questions raised. I can only imagine the thrill, relief, and pride she must have felt at this subtle airing of a twenty-two-year-old secret. If people did, in fact, question or puzzle over or whisper about the wording of the invitation, it happened behind my back and I never heard a word.

My father, of course, was not a forgettable businessman from Pennsylvania. He was in my life from the start.

+ + +

On Sundays, my mother often made us a special breakfast of *naleśniki*, thin Polish crêpes with butter and jelly, covered with cinnamon sugar, or, if the butcher had them, sautéed lamb kidneys that we'd carefully skinned, halved, and soaked all night in salted water. Well-dried and rolled in seasoned flour, they were also a favorite breakfast specialty. We dressed with care and then drove to St. Peter's Church in South Norwood.

I loved St. Peter's, a Polish church where the customs and hymns of the old country were practiced and preserved. The pastor, Rev. Hippolyte Zawalich, a vibrant presence known to everyone as Father Hip, was exuberant, dedicated, and beloved by his parishioners. His masses were always crowded on Sunday. He had attended Polish elementary school with our cousins in South Boston and was a special friend of my family. He celebrated two masses on Sundays and they were always crowded.

Father Hip lived next door to the church in a brick, two-story rectory he designed and had built. He decorated the church for all the holidays, trained his altar boys, mowed his lawn, and shoveled the winter snow. He visited all of the houses of his parishioners to bless their food on the eve of Easter, when bread, salt, dairy, fish, and elaborately painted Easter eggs were laid on dining room tables for him to sprinkle with holy water. At the Feast of the Magi, in early January, he blessed the houses by marking the top of each doorframe with three chalk crosses and the letters C, M, and B to symbolize the visit of the three kings—Caspar, Melchior, and Balthasar—to the infant Christ. He baptized the newborns, prepared the children for communion, heard confessions, counseled engaged couples before marriage, conducted weddings and funerals, visited the sick and elderly, and generally presided over his close-knit community and served it well.

It is clear to me now that Father Hip enjoyed being a priest, a demanding vocation with a myriad of parish duties. He especially enjoyed celebrating the Mass. That reenactment of the Last Supper was the heart of his calling. He oversaw the entire operation, from adorning the church the night before with his own flower arrangements to singing the Mass in his clear Latin and preaching his sermon in both Polish and English to a church that was never less than packed. At the end, having successfully staged his sacred drama and having pronounced the words *Ite, missa est* ("Go, the mass is ended"), he could finally relax and enjoy the more mundane hours of his Sunday, devoted to the pleasures of the table.

The best part of my Sunday began with Father Hip's *Ite, missa est*. How I waited to hear those words, particularly on the days when we were invited for breakfast in the rectory around the festive dining table. I'd help Kasia, Father Hip's elderly housekeeper, serve plates of liver sausage (*kiszká*), kielbasa, ham, bacon, toast, eggs, and the fragrant coffee served with babka, a Polish soft bread sprinkled through with dried fruit. Father Hip presided over those breakfasts like an exuberant Bacchus, his ample belly rocking with laughter at the rich fund of stories he and his friends would tell. After breakfast, we'd count the collection. I'd roll coins while the others counted bills, and Father Hip wrote his entries neatly into the parish ledger.

Kasia, in the meantime, would have cleared the kitchen, and we'd fill that room with polka dancing, rocking the kitchenware that was stacked to dry. If that did not satisfy Father Hip's boundless energy, he'd lead us to the ping pong table in the cellar, where he'd whoop in triumph when he smashed an ace drive against a determined but helpless opponent. These festive, uproarious breakfasts were the treat of my week. The conversation was animated, for he was a natural host and popular after-dinner speaker, a storyteller who was always ready with the latest jokes that circulated among the businessmen, politicians, policemen, and, due to his many activities in greater Boston, a wide circle of friends and acquaintances.

Father Hip was my guardian and special friend. It would be

many years before I understood the irony of the name I called him by: Pate, short for *pater*, the Latin word for father.

✦ ✦ ✦

NORWOOD

My hometown of Norwood, with its population of roughly fifteen thousand souls, would make a fine model for anyone interested in the social dynamics of a New England mill town of the mid-twentieth century. The earliest settlers had lived in the area adjacent to Dedham in the seventeenth century, but the town was not formally established until 1872, by which time it had missed out on the classic aesthetic that had imprinted itself on the look and layout of earlier New England towns. Though its site lacked a river to provide the energy for a large complex of textile mills like those in Lawrence or Lowell, Norwood became the home of the Plimpton Press, the Kendall Mills, and the Winslow Tannery; Bird & Son, a large roofing and siding company, had its base in nearby Walpole. The town was strung out loosely along the railroad tracks that provided freight access for these businesses, whose workers came out of the immigrant Irish, Italian, Finnish, Polish, Lithuanian, and Syrian communities, each with its own neighborhood and a church at its physical and spiritual center. Finally, add to these the well-to-do WASPs who hired the diverse immigrant population to work in their mills and their large houses as housekeepers, gardeners, and nursemaids.

Washington Street (Route 1A) was the main artery of Norwood in the 1940s and '50s. A direct line between home, school, and church, it was also the central axis of my childhood: my first eighteen years were passed at significant stops on its progress through the town.

The house where my mother and I lived was located where Washington entered Norwood from neighboring Westwood.

On school-day mornings, I walked the half mile that separated our house from St. Catherine's School, past an open field and tidy neighborhood houses to the edge of the business district of town. At the lunch break, I proceeded past the open vegetable market, the taxi stand, and the newsstand to my mother's beauty shop, located above a block of small stores. At the end of the town center, Washington Street forked to the left, leading to the junior high school and hospital, then passed the mills and moved under the railroad bridge into South Norwood, or "The Flats." Here you found triple-decker housing, various churches that anchored the ethnic communities of first- and second-generation Lithuanian, Syrian, and Polish families, and a string of markets, bars, and service businesses, including the Jewish bakery where we went on Fridays for crusty, warm-from-the-oven rye bread. Nestled at the edge of town, just before Washington Street left Norwood and entered Walpole, was the Polish settlement and its Catholic church— our church, St. Peter's, presided over by Father Hip.

Washington Street was the axis of my town and my childhood. My mother and I lived at one end of the street, went to church at the other end, and in the middle went our separate ways to work and school. As my son recently pointed out, the two ends of the street were the poles of Norwood's main thoroughfare, and also, at the same two extremities, were located the two Poles of my world—my mother and Father Hip.

✦ ✦ ✦

Father Hip had been our friend for as long as I could remember. My first memory of him is early one evening at our house when Alice was still alive, so I must have been five. A group of people were on the front porch and I had been promised a treat. Father Hip arrived with several quarts of ice cream, something I loved. When the cartons were opened, I was horrified to see the ice cream was green! As a special treat he had brought pistachio, and in my

Father Hip, ca. 1954

mind he might have brought boiled turnips. Bitterly disappointed, I refused to taste it. I have rarely eaten nut ice cream since. It is an ironic first memory of someone I came to adore—and whose characteristic trait and great pleasure was to provide abundance.

After Alice died, I saw Father Hip more often. He came to dinner at our house, sometimes several times a week, sometimes arriving laden with special foods from the open markets in Boston's North End. He'd pull his car in the straight driveway that ran close to the side of our house, and come in the side door that led directly into our kitchen, where he'd settle at the dining table, relaxing over a martini. My mother would prepare something simple like swordfish, baked potato, and broccoli, and I would assemble a salad. I remember nothing about what we said during those evenings. Afterwards, in my room doing homework, I could hear the low sounds of their conversation, often conducted in Polish. An hour or two later I'd hear the door to the back stairs close, and after a while I would hear his car start under my bedroom window. My mother would wash the dishes as she listened to the radio or to her collection of classical records, and I went to sleep to Chopin, Tchaikovsky, or Wagner.

Polish was the background music of my childhood. Like the now mostly discarded Latin Mass, its sounds were familiar and comforting, but at the same time it was mysterious. It was the language my parents used when conversing alone or speaking of things they didn't want me to know. As I grew older, I absorbed enough Polish to recognize the stories being told around me, but I could not speak it and, in fact, was not encouraged to do so. I was the only one in my extended maternal family who did not speak our ancestral language, and I see now that it was another way I was set apart. Pate did teach me to say the Polish Hail Mary and Our Father, but that was the extent of my knowledge.

I spent a lot of time with Pate after school and on weekends when my mother was working. In the fall and spring, he'd pick me up after school a few times a week, bringing his Springer spaniel, Rags, and we'd head to his fishing shack on Norwood's Willet's Pond. We'd park at the Fish and Game Club, which leased his fishing shack, and put his little outboard motor into his rowboat, which he'd dubbed the "Beamy Mimi." Loaded up, we'd head out to the jutting spit of land where the shack was set. Alternatively, we could park farther along the road and walk to the shack via the fields along the side of the pond, with Rags barking ahead of us. I loved either approach. At the camp, which sported a porch, a cot, a rudimentary kitchen, and an outhouse, I'd change and rush out for a swim. Pate did his chores—a bit of carpentry, raking leaves, ti-dying—and came down to join me by the water, enjoying the sun. On cooler days we'd shoot targets or go out fishing, using for bait the night crawlers we'd hunted with flashlights on our lawn. We skipped stones and counted the rings; we tinkered with the little green one-horsepower outboard motor. We went rowing around an island in the middle of the pond, and, eventually, he would row and I would swim longer and longer distances. Later, I'd take the rowboat out alone to explore the coves and inlets, where there were polliwogs and painted turtles enough to survive my hunting expeditions. I saw and was transfixed by great blue herons, which seemed unconcerned with my small, invading self. It was a dream realm for a child that I ruled serenely. Father Hip had a whistle; he blew it if I became too deeply absorbed in my explorations, and I returned at once.

In the fall, Father Hip and I would gather wild mushrooms for his mother to preserve. Like all avid mushroom hunters, he had never-to-be-divulged picking places, located along dirt roads on the Bird Estate in Walpole. He'd park the car in the middle of the dirt road and we would walk ahead, me fanning out looking for mushrooms for him to pick or reject. When we got far enough along, he would say, "Okay, Scout, go get the car and bring it here." Probably twelve or thirteen years old by then, I would go back and cautiously move the car forward. It was a daunting request, but I did it with care as he nonchalantly walked in front of me.

Father Hip shared a larger, wonderful world with me, from those dirt roads to the dusty antique shops of the South End to, once, a thrillingly impromptu trip to Quebec. I loved these adventures and would go anywhere with him.

✦ ✦ ✦

Once, after a mushroom hunt, Pate took me to his family home in Dorchester to deliver the mushrooms to his mother. A small lady, she had silken white hair in a soft bun, with kind snappy eyes framed by round, silver-rimmed eyeglasses. Her secret indulgence, I learned later, was to bet on the greyhounds at the dog track. Though she had been born in Boston, her son Hippolyte was born in Poland while she was there visiting relatives. She had raised seven children, of whom Father Hip was her eldest and her pride.

✦ ✦ ✦

While I have few memories of, Mary, Pate's mother, my maternal relatives loomed large. Intrepid, resourceful women were the models, the power source, the heroines of the Czarnecki family story. My grandmother and her siblings came at the beginning of the twentieth century to the East Coast of the United States from Poland. They were the four elder sisters in a family of five brothers and five sisters, a family literally blasted apart by World War I. I wonder about their mother, Paulina (Moszkiewicz) Czarnecki, the matriarch and, I sense, the source of the intrepid drive and energy that characterized the four sisters I grew up with: Michalina, Alexandra (Alice), Stefania, and Adeline. These women spoke very little about their childhood in Poland. They came one at a time to this country and got on with the business of working in the textile mills of Lawrence, Massachusetts, marrying and making their way in the United States. Displaying the mettle of their indomitable mother, they soon settled among the close-knit Polish community in Boston's Dorchester neighborhood. The men they married were, like my mild grandfather, incidental witnesses to their drive and personalities.

In a formal portrait, my great-grandmother, Paulina, is seated with her husband, Jòzef, and two of her five sons, one in a cadet's uniform. Her forceful will comes through in her direct gaze at the camera. My great-grandfather, a dreamy mild man beloved by his

Paulina Czarnecki and family

children, was the head gamekeeper of the tsar's hunting grounds, located in a section of northeast Poland that was still part of the Russian empire.

Paulina was the daughter of a prosperous butcher when she met Jòzef. The village where they married and settled down is in northeast Poland on land granted to Jòzef's noble forebear, Stefan Czarniecki, a hero of Poland whose name is mentioned in the Polish national anthem. The whole district had been given to Stefan in the seventeenth century by the king of Poland in return for his victories as a military commander. So Paulina married into an august if, by then, much diminished branch of the family.

One suspects she made the most of this connection as she evidently became the "go to" person in the village and eventually became a sort of private moneylender. When the family decided to flee Poland, she provided a packet of her carefully hoarded Russian rubles for their escape to India through Turkey and Iran. Her family soon discovered that her rubles were worthless, and they used them to light a fire under their tea kettle when they made camp. Paulina, too old and sick to make the arduous trek, had elected to remain in Poland. She died in Troszyn in 1939.

During a trip to Poland in 1985 with my cousin Lidia Granski, I met Aunt Helena, the youngest of the Czarnecki sisters, the one who hadn't emigrated. She lived in a remote village with no telephone service and so we were unable to warn her of our coming. And yet we arrived to find the family expecting us and with a feast

Lidia and me in a field of Polish lupine

prepared. It seems that an old woman in the village had alerted our cousins that they should expect visitors from far away! In her late nineties, Aunt Helena was still a force of nature, moving among her elderly children, staying with them for as long as they could put up with her. At the feast, she stood at the head of the table and raised her vodka glass to sing the Polish toasting song "Sto lat!" It was an uncanny experience to meet this ancient woman for the first time and find her so familiar.

+ + +

Of the four Czarnecki sisters who emigrated to America from Poland at the turn of the twentieth century, Alexandra, known to all as Alice, was the most determined to learn English, educate herself, and become Americanized. Her English was fluent, not halting and heavily accented like that of her sisters, who persisted in speaking Polish in their families. My own recollections of her are, of course, those of a small child. I remember, for instance, sitting in her lap as a toddler. I looked out the window, saw an airplane, and said the word "airplane." Alice was astonished that I knew the word—after all it was 1938 and airplanes were not common sights. What a smart child I was, she exclaimed!—and I learned that using my brain earned points.

Those who knew Alice speak of her great charm and forceful personality, her unconventional chain smoking, and her beautiful clothes. She was invariably the center of any gathering and was usually deep in conversation with a circle of men. She adored the ocean and I retain her conviction that it is healing to bathe in salt water. Most of the remaining images of her are set by the ocean, on Cape Cod or aboard ship. She loved children to the degree that my generation in the family all recall a sense of being cherished in her presence. That her own daughter, Florence, endured a bleak and lonely childhood remains an unanswered and ironic family mystery.

Alice, my grandmother

After arriving in the States, Alice had met and married a fellow Polish immigrant in Lawrence, but they were soon separated when he went off to fight in the First World War. Robert Fojuth was a handsome man about whom little is known, other than that he was a lady's man. Their daughter, Florence, was born in 1911. Foyette is the Anglicized version of Fojuth; Alice began using it after their separation.

Robert Foyuth, my grandfather

Florence and Alice,
Hyannis, Masschusetts,
ca. 1934

I know few details of Alice's early drive as a single mother to establish herself as a businesswoman. I *do* know that her ambition and need to support her daughter required her to leave Florence for long periods during the hard years when she worked to acquire rental properties that were subsequently lost during the Great Depression. Florence had stayed during these times with her aunts, and for several years was sent to board with nuns in Lowell. Her lonely letters to Alice that exist from that period are brief, somber, and correct. Perhaps recalling this neglect of her daughter Florence, forced on her by monetary circumstances, Alice was determined to lavish on me all her natural love of children. I was pampered and cherished to the fullest extent. In our family each of the four sisters had one or two daughters who never married and lived on with their mothers. Consequently, I was received into an extended family made up primarily of women and doted on as the only baby.

Alice's charming, outgoing nature had another side. Like her sisters, she possessed a strong matriarchal streak and so kept a tight emotional rein on Florence, who attracted constant attention from suitors who threatened to take her away. Afraid of a lonely old age in those days before decent facilities for the elderly, Alice invariably staged a health crisis, demanding that Florence not leave her.

Alice and Florence had launched Alice's Beauty Shop after losing their real estate rental properties. Witnessing the success of Helena Rubenstein and Elizabeth Arden, pioneers in the beauty industry, the entrepreneurial Alice saw a niche in hairdressing after the First World War, and the shop had thrived. Later on, after Alice's death, Florence took over the running of the shop, maintaining a core clientele of loyal customers through the years.

I spent most of my childhood afternoons in the shop, taking in the array of intriguing feminine processes and operations that my mother presided over. It was the era of the electric permanent wave, and it wasn't unusual to find her customers seated happily in what would look now like a torture device, their hair in heated rollers that were clamped to electric wires, which hung down from an overhead stand. One woman insisted on the long-outdated Marcel hairstyle, so my mother hot-tonged her tresses and kept her looking like an aging 1920s silent-film star. I can still smell the Zotoz chemicals, the hot wax, and the formaldehyde she used to sanitize her combs.

Schooldays I spent in the classrooms and corridors of the St. Catherine of Siena School, where the Sisters of St. Joseph pounded knowledge into the sturdy children of immigrants—mainly Irish but with a smattering of Italian, Polish, Syrian, and Lithuanian. In five rows of desks, eight children per row, the children of doctors and lawyers were instructed alongside the children of laborers and small-business owners. We studied history, geography, and art (which consisted of coloring in blue images on multigraphed sheets). We learned our religion from the Baltimore Catechism, a series of questions and answers we had to memorize. Who made the world? God made the world. Does God know all things? God knows all things, even our most secret thoughts, words, and actions.

Sister Alcantara, with some of my classmates, ca. 1948

✦ ✦ ✦

I spent two months each summer at Camp Bonheur on New Hampshire's Lake Winnipesaukee. Edna Payne, my mother's customer and friend, had a daughter who was a camp counselor there, so my mother felt secure in packing me off for two months starting at the age of six. I loved camp, and eight years later, after Bonheur closed, I spent two summers at Camp Kineowatha in Wilton, Maine. Safely on my own and, being a tomboy, in my element, I took eagerly to the outdoor life, with its daily regimen of swimming, archery, tennis, riflery, and boating, along with play productions, campfires, camp-outs, and rainy days spent in the big boathouse playing games and puzzles. We were required to send weekly letters home; those missives and the written responses we received were our only contact with our families.

A Letter from Pate to Camper Mimi

St. Peter's Rectory
27 St. Joseph's Ave.
Norwood, Mass.

Mimi Alexandra Foyette
Camp Kineowatha
Wilton, Maine

August 20, 1951

Dear Mimi —

. . . I am very glad that I could give you this month—believe you me. You're still my best girl—true you irritate, nag, abuse me but as I always said—less time in purgatory "old man." Of course when *we* grow older we become more impatient with young people who have ceased to be cute, and become young ladies. For two reasons:

first because the years (darn those 39) separating us as time goes on, make us oldies lose perspective and understanding of the young people's point of view *occasionally only* and then we become gruff ruff and nasty. But needless to say we hurt the youngster and irritate ourselfs (of course with my angelic disposition I have no trouble thataway). Secondly: this *is* important—we (the oldies) have made all the same mistakes & errors you are bound to make. We too were embarrassed—we cried over spilt milk—we were angered to tears. Some of us fell by the wayside because of these mistakes and errors because no one was around to correct them. Now because of this experience we see the signs of danger more clearly—(a man who touches a red hot stove once with his finger never tries it again) we try to warn—but where youth triumphant scorns the warning we become impatient irritable and unbearable (sometimes) for we see pitfall and the consequences. So much for philosophy. How is your love life—are there any new men around Kineawatha! Friends of friends or brothers of sisters? Or is the camp still a maidenly haven pure, prim, and prissy with only old "chicks" to love. It better be!

Well darling my eyes are tired. I had a hard day. . . . Thanks for your prayers. Never forget them, sometimes whisper an Ave to our Lady for your old

Pate.

Lord love you—sweet dreams Chicken

8/10-/51

Festus St. Laurenti

+ + +

As a young child I didn't wonder about who my birth parents might be or what had happened to them. But as I grew older, I felt bewildered and isolated as I began to be aware of what being adopted really meant and implied: something neither easy to convey nor easy for a child to go on taking for granted. Questions arise, however much one is loved and cherished. Who am I really? Why was I given up for adoption? What was wrong with me? Where is my other/real family? Are they alive? If I don't measure up, will I be sent back? This last question was quite inadvertently but painfully underlined when I was about eleven years old.

Late one afternoon, as it was growing dark, my mother, tired and ready to close her shop for the day, became alarmed at my uncharacteristic failure to return. She began calling the local shopkeepers to ask if they had seen me. I appeared on my roller skates not long after, but by that time she was alarmed enough to have alerted Father Hip. It was an innocent misstep on my part, and it is not her reaction but Father Hip's that is seared in my memory.

As much as I reveled in Pate's high spirits and sense of fun, I feared his disapproval. He was eloquent and severe when angered. The day after my late homecoming, he came in his car to pick me up after school and then took me for a drive out of town. He did not reveal where we were headed; there was only a stern lecture followed by a long tension-filled silence. Finally, we entered a gate onto a private drive leading to a large brick building. The omnipresent blue plaster statue of the Virgin Mary in its little garden tipped me off that it was a religious institution of some sort.

The nun who answered the doorbell was evidently expecting us. I have a strong memory of dark paneled walls and the pungent woody fragrance of polished furniture and highly waxed floors, and of the hush that settled in as we waited in a formal reception room. Soon a tall, older nun, the mother superior, came in and greeted Father Hip. He introduced us and proceeded to tell her in detail that I was a naughty child who had frightened my mother. I was made to understand, in no uncertain terms, that should I repeat my recent thoughtless behavior, the reverend mother was very willing to take me back into what I now realized was an orphanage. As with other traumatic moments in my life, I remember nothing beyond the awful moment of comprehending the full import of the threat. My world had come crashing down, and my safety and security could no longer be taken for granted.

I was a bright and high-spirited child, good-natured, well-behaved, the sort the nuns tended to favor. I was also sensitive and this enormous and terrifying threatened punishment for a simple mistake, wholly innocent on my part, crushed me. Some little fire went out that day because I had seen with my own eyes the consequences of an error, and knew that I could lose everything and *be sent back*. I had been adopted by two women, and now the father figure I most loved and relied on was prepared to treat me like unsatisfactory goods. It was a threat that worsened an already difficult set of circumstances for an eleven-year-old, one that for many years dampened my innate sense of risk and adventure. I no longer had any margin for failure. I, who loved to climb trees and read there in comfort, was now perched at the end of a dry limb.

Father Hip could not begin to imagine what this vividly dramatized threat would mean to a child who knew herself to be adopted. He knew who I was and his sense of himself was rock solid. He knew his family, his forebears, his siblings, and his place as the favored oldest son in the order of things. My sense of myself was built on sand that now had turned to dangerous quicksand. My circumstances were utterly unlike those of all the children I knew in school or encountered in summer camp. How could I answer ordinary questions easily?

—*What does your father do?*

—*I don't have one.*

—*Why?*

Pate had no sense of the emotional, let alone the linguistic, confusions of my situation. Psychology was practically still in utero, Freud barely dead and Jung still alive. I learned not to ask questions but to watch and listen for clues and nuances, and not even to speculate about my reality. It all got buried down deep inside: secrets, mysteries, confusions, and thoughts not to be thought, feelings not to be felt. I developed hair-trigger antennae for the subtle pitfalls of life around me.

Pate's punishment did not generate in me a sense of betrayal or rebellious anger, imbued as I was by the nuns with a sense of responsibility and guilt. They had trained us to "offer up" our sorrow to the Blessed Mother, and so I duly offered it up and resolved to do better. I certainly bore no resentment against Father Hip; my relationship with him continued as usual. He clearly cared for me, and soon the memory of this frightening event slipped into my subconscious. It did not reappear until I was in therapy some thirty years later.

✦ ✦ ✦

In eighth grade, I won a scholarship to Holy Cross Academy, a new Catholic girls' day school in Brookline run by the Holy Cross nuns. In the mornings, our next-door neighbor, Ernie Wohler, dropped me off at the academy on his way to Tufts Medical School. His carpool, which included a rotating uproar of two or three other med students from Norwood, served as my introduction to condensed male energy. In deference to this uniformed high-school girl, they suppressed their more ribald medical school humor until I was let off at Holy Cross.

I eventually dated all of those medical students in rotation, which likely prompted the following notice from Father Hip.

Pate's Rules for Dates at 335 Washington

School Year: Only <u>Fridays</u> and <u>Saturdays</u>

1) Saturday nite dates: all home work for Monday must be done Sat. before date, <u>not</u> Saturday night, when you're tired.

2) All men must be brought home and introduced to mother at least one time <u>before</u> date if not previously known by her.

3) All dates end at the Cinderella hour on your doorstep. (midnight) 12 pm. NO ifs, ors or buts. Before accepting a date please make this clearly and distinctly understood by the men.

4) Permission for dates will be granted <u>only when</u> all your other obligations do not interfere [with] your scholastic standing, the order and care of the home, your religious obligations and your family.

5) Permission for dates expresses complete trust in your maturity. An infringement of these rules states openly that you are not ready for that trust and all dates shall be immediately cancelled until such a time when in the opinion of your mother, you have learned to appreciate the privilege!

Holy Cross Academy provided a contrast to the no-nonsense St. Catherine's parochial school. Set on the grounds of two adjoining estates, the school's classes were held in a mansion. Its black shutters were overhung in the spring with a wisteria vine that covered the front of the building and sent through the open windows a fragrance that diverted even the most studious of us. Unlike the tough, drillmaster nuns of St. Catherine's, the easygoing young Holy Cross nuns were full of fun.

Sister Canisius, the mother superior, spoke with an enfolding drawl from her Atlanta background. She established a culture in that school that was kind and civilized. She made no objection when I chose not to visit the many Catholic colleges in the area, but instead considered Vassar, Bryn Mawr, Mount Holyoke, and Smith. I opted for the latter on the lofty basis of its swimming pool and my admiration of my summer camp counselors, who were largely Smith students.

The nuns had stressed that only very special souls were given a vocation, that it was God's highest calling. For several years they had been urging me to consider joining their order, tagging me as one of those special souls. They appealed to my idealism, and were successful to the extent that my mother drove me out at spring vacation of my senior year to the mother house in South Bend, Indiana, where I was welcomed and shown its world. My wise mother did not openly object to this plan, but on the drive back after our visit she made a deal with me. "Mimi, you have a scholarship. You go to Smith and we will reconsider this plan at the end of your freshman year." Off I went to Smith and, with the first invasion of Yale men, that conversation reconsidering the convent never happened.

PART TWO

Keeping a secret . . . is much like sitting on a time bomb.
Powerful events initiate the need to keep a secret, but once
kept the secret itself becomes an explosive device.

—TOM COTTLE, *Children's Secrets*

SMITH COLLEGE

I LANDED LIKE AN ALIEN in the formidable if friendly women's college in the fall of 1954, knowing not one soul in my incoming class and taken off-guard by an attack of homesickness when my mother drove off. Northampton, Massachusetts, a college town overlaid with cultural history, offered numerous restaurants and cafés and an excellent bookstore. Cheery groups of girls already knew one another from Kent Place, Brearly, and Miss Porter's schools, and cliques from Houston and Cleveland buzzed around campus. I was set apart as a Catholic, as a scholarship student, and as a singleton from a small mill town. But I did not feel the isolation for long. Carried along in this bustle like a plastic bag in wind-blown leaves, I eventually found my place, landing in a congenial circle of friends that included two who had, like me, been adopted.

✦ ✦ ✦

Sometime during the fall of my freshman year, Father Hip announced he was coming for a visit, and suggested gathering a group of my friends for a festive meal. Eager to see me in place at college and laden with goodies from the Boston grocer and importer S. S. Pierce, he swept me and my friends off to Wiggins Tavern, the favored restaurant in Northampton for special occasions. He was in his element providing bounty and, with his fund of energy and his teasing, made such an indelible impression on my friends that they remembered that occasion years later. I don't remember the specifics of what we ate or what we talked about, but I was excited to show off my charming guardian priest to my friends.

That's my last memory of Father Hip, though I must have seen him over Christmas break. He had suffered a stroke the previous year, and for a time had pulled away, emotionally and physically. My mother explained it as a side effect of the stroke; still, it caused some distress in our home. But once I was off to Smith, wading through an overload of survey courses, my thoughts were elsewhere. Soon, Pate was writing me again and seemed like his old self.

Excerpt from a letter from Father Hip
October 22, 1954

I hope you knocked all your tests for "a loop." Don't expect too much however. It is pretty hard to grow up overnight. I remember I had a tremendous time getting accustomed to regulating my life when I went away to school. The transition from youth to maturity is a big step. You are expected to do so much it becomes baffling at first. Everyone tries to do too much in trying to live up to the glamour of college life. Some stay with the glamour and forget all else. Others find that happy medium between the real, serious study and the wonderful social opportunities college offers.

It takes at least one term to learn how much time you can spend on your social activities without hurting your scholastic progress.

It takes at least one term to adjust yourself to the new ways of teaching—dashing from building to building—from class to library, from seminar to discussion group.

It takes at least one term to learn and get accustomed to studying in your room with the tremendous amount of distractions surrounding you.

Then from this utter confusion, suddenly you will learn to evaluate and coordinate. You will develop a sense of timing. (How much time you can sacrifice socially + how much you must devote to your studies.) Once that personal equation is arrived at you'll be happy.

You can't kid on this subject. You only kid yourself if you do. College says here are the fruits of opportunity—but—you—and only you can pick them.

Yes, it's hard to decide what to pick—how to pick and how much to store—when to pic becomes important also or we can overburden our selfs.

All this sounds ominous, baffling, and discouraging—but don't worry. It took even the good Lord seven days to create the world. Don't think that you can conquer Smith in seven weeks.

All these things I wrote are important but to me the most important thing in college life was prayer—over one of the portals of a study hall they had these words chiseled in granite: "ora et labora," pray + work. Please believe me it is a wonderful motto for any serious student. A decade of the rosary has frequently solved problems the tired human brain was confused by. Prayer, daily prayer, gives strength, hope, clarity of understanding and courage to go on when hopelessly we are confused—tired—and let down.

The Blessed mother is always at your side, giving you a part of her strength—her clarity of understanding and a solution. Like a benevolent mother here She whispers "Now do the best you can. I'll see about the rest." So when tired, in doubt—when discouraged—when you need a lift, turn to Her. She's constantly waiting to help.

And so, "slugsy," keep your chin up and keep punching. Rome wasn't built in a day—and don't think you'd be competing with Confucius if you took Chinese for seven weeks.

Do the best you can—Pray—and take each
day as it comes, one at a time—before you scale
Everest you have to conquer the valleys.

God bless you and give you strength. I know
you have it. Wait until you get rolling. Then you'll
show them. I love you.

Today, with the benefit of time and parenthood and secure in the
knowledge that my *Pater,* my capital "F" Father, was also my small
"f" father, I read this letter imagining that he is trying to tell me
something of his own loss and regret: all those years of reciting
the rosary, *Hail Mary, full of grace,* of turning to the Blessed Mother
rather than the perhaps less understanding Father Almighty of the
Catholic Church. I can only imagine the doubts he must have faced
daily as he tried to do his best for his unacknowledged family,
knowing that to publicly embrace us would mean leaving behind
everything else he knew and cared about.

Long before the days of genetic testing, when spitting into a
vial and mailing it off to a genealogy website can reveal secrets un-
told back several generations, Pate must have realized that I might
eventually fill in the puzzle pieces, or that someone else might reveal the truth of our family tree. Perhaps he even looked forward
to a day when he might tell me himself. Might he have told me
when he presided at my wedding? Had he lived just three more
years, he would have had that opportunity.

But we never had the chance to know each other as father and
daughter. In May of 1955, near the end of my freshman year, I was
abruptly called home during the exam period. Father Hip had died
suddenly. He was only forty-seven.

✦ ✦ ✦

NORWOOD MESSENGER, TUESDAY, MAY 5, 1955

Final Tribute Paid Beloved Pastor of St. Peter's Today

With more than 200 members of the parish and friends of the Rev. Hippolyte J. Zawalich unable to gain admission to the church, final tribute was paid this morning to the beloved pastor of St. Peter's Polish Church, South Norwood, who died suddenly Monday night at the age of 47.

Bishop Jeremiah F. Minihan of St. Catherine's Church presided at the Solemn High Requiem Mass. Celebrant was the Rev. Edward Wayuszenski of Hyde Park. Deacon was Rev. John Dziok of East Cambridge; sub-deacon was Rev. William Maciaszek of Hyde Park; master of ceremonies, Rev. L. A. Ciesirisker of Ipswich; eulogist, Rt. Rev. Ladislaw A. Sikora of salem; the cross bearer, Rev. Ferdinand Slejzer of Lowell; acolytes, Rev. Frank Chrag of the West End and Rev. Francis S. Miaskiewicz of Maynard; thurifer, Rev. C. J. Stempkowak of Hyde Park, and boat bearer, Rev. J. Weber Stocklosa of East Cambridge.

Seated within the church for the mass were more than 25 other priests who came from Lowell, Haverhill, Lawrence, Emmanuel College, Boston, Clairmont, N.H., Maynard, and Brookline to pay their last respects to the Norwood Parish Priest.

Representing the town of Norwood were Town Manager John B. Kennedy, Town Clerk Walter A. Blasenak, and two members of the Board of Selectmen, Chairman Daniel E. Callahan and Harry B. Butters. The Chamber of Commerce was represented by Secretary Arthur V. Wilson. Representing the State Police was Major George Alexander, and Capt. Arthur O'Leary. A detail of Norwood police was led by Chief Mark Folan.

An honorary guard of four members of Fourth Degree, Knights of Columbus, represented the Norwood K. of C. They were: Dr. Timothy J. Curtin, Town Counsel Francis Foley, Lee Richardson, and Mark Coyne.

As the bell on the ancient church tolled, the procession proceeded from the adjacent rectory to the church where the body of Fr. Zawalich already lay in state in front of the altar. The choir which sang at the funeral was from St. John's Seminary, where Fr. Zawalich had prepared for the priesthood.

All of the curates of St. Catherine's Church—Rev. William Maguire, Rev. William Carroll, Rev. Joseph MacDonald, and Rev. Tichard O'Halloran—were in attendance. Rev. Felix Norbut, Pastor, and Rev. Joseph J. Svirskas, assistant, represented the neighboring St. George's Lithuanian Church. Rev. Thomas Condon, pastor of St. Margaret Mary's Church, Westwood, was present. All of the Polish societies were officially represented at the funeral services.

The limited seating capacity of the church allowed only members of the clergy, town officials, official society delegates, and members of the family to crowd within the church edifice. Others remained outside on the steps and on grounds while the mass was in progress.

The funeral cortege left St. Joseph avenue for Forest Hills where burial took place in St. Michael's Cemetery.

Death came suddenly Monday night to the popular priest who had served the local Polish parish for 21 years. Born in Poland, Fr. Zawalich had come to this country with his parents at an early age. He was ordained to the priesthood in 1932 by the late Cardinal O'Connell.

Fr. Zawalich is survived by his mother, Mrs. Mary Zawalich of Dorchester; four sisters, Miss Helen Zawalich of Dorchester, Mrs. Anna M. Piasta of Webster, Mrs. Edna Kundzicz of Virginia, and Mrs. Phyllis Harrelson of Virginia, and two brothers, Albert and Edmund of Dorchester.

✦ ✦ ✦

Though the weeks following it have retreated into sepia in my memory, Father Hip's funeral still plays there like a brilliant video clip. On the warm May morning, St. Peter's Church, where he'd served for twenty years and which was a second home for me, was filled beyond capacity with seated dignitaries and with parishioners lined up against the walls and outside crowding the entrance and gathered in the street beyond. The sanctuary was adorned with wreaths and sprays of flowers. I sat in the third or fourth row on the right side; Pate's closed casket sat in the center aisle. Several priests and a monsignor celebrated the funeral mass, and when it came time for the pallbearers to roll the casket down the middle aisle, at the moment when he was taken irrevocably away, I began to sob. All restraint and caution deserted me, and someone, I don't remember who, immediately muffled me, moved me quickly to the side door, and then half marched, half carried me to the rectory. I did not (could not?) go to the cemetery, and I remember nothing of the days and months that followed. Did I return to college to take final exams? My college friends, when I asked them in later years, could not recall. Did I work that summer? What of my mother, and what did we talk about? How did we make it through those summer months? Did we talk about his death as we retreated into our private sorrow? I think not. I think it all went into a black hole of denial to be packed away with all the other taboo subjects.

> **Journal entry, February 24, 1991:** In the worst trauma of my young life, I had no way to recover and no way to express my feelings, and indeed a very tight lid was placed on them. . . . When my father died, I had no legitimate right to grieve, to sit within the family circle, and at that moment I had lost the key to my identity. At some level I knew

he would never now be able to look at me and say, *You are my child.* I went on without grieving, with a kind of amnesia fog to mask the pain and drive it inside. Not consciously aware of who he was, I went on and began periods of depression, walking the floors at night at Smith, terrified of failing and losing my education, of being a failure for my mother, and not knowing what the pain was all about. I never got to say goodbye to him.

And so it began. Four months after his death, in the fall of my sophomore year, I found myself beset by a new and troubling problem, an ailment I did not have the word for. Nor did I know that there were college psychologists who might have helped me to deal with an unmourned death and with my unexpressed grief. It was the onset of what would grow into years of intermittent, sometimes severe, and eventually suicidal depression. I was on my own and simply had to get on with my coursework and my life.

Four months after Father Hip's death, I wrote to my mother from Lamont House, my dormitory.

I really have had a very hard month since I have been back at college and I'm just beginning now to come out from a very low mental state. It comes in cycles and I get low over Pater and worry about you so much. I think we both sit and worry about the other more than we should. I hadn't slept at night and I couldn't work and it became a vicious circle. I was behind in my work and sleep and too far ahead in my worry. I've been worried about you, about my marks, about my work, about my work in Newman Club, about my laundry, about my very purpose in life and I got submerged in this and forgot all other.

It reached a peak last week and my written exams unfortunately were scheduled for then and they all suffered. I got my first D. Miss Lowry has been wonderful to me and has been giving me pills to sleep occasionally and I am beginning to come out of it all. I feel much better for merely having written it all down. I didn't have anyone to talk to and it's impossible over the phone. I was in the mail hall of Lamont today and was trying to talk with you and fight tears and keep the other people out of our conversation. It was quite impossible. I'm not at all pressed for time now and can get caught up. I'm behind in everything. I have five Greek plays, Machiavelli's work and Aristotle and Byron and Shelley to read for this week alone. Plus my reading in English History. I'm calmed down and am sorry that this all came to a head as it did. I've been so beside myself that I haven't done anything about writing or anything to anybody.

Please be assured that today was a turning point and don't worry about me from here on in. I'm very happy at Lamont and very interested in my work but these other thoughts undermined it and ruined the last month. This letter has done me no end of good and I hope it puts your mind at ease so that we can talk it out Friday.

What I did not know, and therefore could not sympathize with, was the extent of my mother's loss. Father Hip was the love of her life. In my letter I see my efforts to ease her worry, but she must have been concerned that I might lose my scholarship if my grades continued to suffer. I assume she had relied on Father Hip to help with my college fees, a burden she now carried alone. What's more, all their dreams for me, everything they worked for, were starting to take me away from her. I began accepting invitations to spend Thanksgivings and spring vacations away from Norwood, with my college friends. She never protested, but rather delighted in hearing about my adventures when I came home.

✦ ✦ ✦

I wrote to my mother that I had come out of my "low mental state," and I did manage to find the balance of schoolwork and social life that my father had urged me to seek out. In my sophomore year at Smith, my group of friends expanded, and I was lucky to find myself among a congenial group of women who would become lifelong friends.

My background and experience, while very different from theirs, was nevertheless supplemented by high spirits and intelligence. I was good company and someone they could safely fix up on double dates with their male friends. Soon I was on the Yale circuit and was eventually able to avoid the cattle auction mixers with the neighboring men's colleges. I recently found a collection of notes from brave boys, saying *I was the one you danced with from Amherst. Would you like to go out next weekend?* We women had to wait to be asked, but I now sympathize with the boys who had the tougher job of initiating contact and risking potential rejection. On many blind dates, I knew instantly that it was likely to be a wasted evening, something to be endured civilly, which was especially trying if an unfinished English paper was awaiting my attention.

We did not all confine ourselves to steady boyfriends, though some of our classmates were "pinned" or engaged. Having grown up among women, my total ignorance of men's anatomy or of their hormonal urges is not surprising. Michelangelo's David was my only frame of reference. Sex was not widely discussed and, at the time, was certainly not graphically portrayed on movie screens where rules dictated that anyone near a bed had to be clothed with their feet on the floor. Lots of erotic innuendo but no action. We assumed that there were "fast" girls men dated for action and "nice" girls they took care of and considered as possible wives. I fell into the latter category. I was a Catholic, so knew punishment for fast behavior was severe. Birth control was not an option. I am not so certain, having observed the freedom that the pill and an open sex life has engendered, which is the better way. Perhaps some of both. Though I can, I admit, think of a number of beaux with whom I should have loved to have had sex, I was always "nice" and always safe. I came safely through a busy four years of dating life.

At Smith College on the bank of Paradise Pond
watching a crew race with my friends, ca. 1957

In those years, Smith College had a faculty of distinguished scholars. As an English major, I was taught by Eliot scholar Elizabeth Drew, Melville biographer Newton Arvin, American Lit scholar and critic Robert Gorham Davis, Russian Lit professor George Gibian, and Shakespeare professor Esther Cloudman Dunne, among many other superb teachers. We were inspired by them, we were challenged, we worked very hard to meet their standards, and, no doubt, to gain their attention. For me, they were a race of people I had not encountered before. I thrived on their tutoring and their accessibility.

My nonacademic life also extended into a variety of student clubs and campus organizations. I joined the Newman Club for Catholic students, was active in student government in my junior year, and became head of the Honor Board. I believe it was on behalf of one of these organizations that I was sent one day to interview Sylvia Plath.

By the time I arrived on campus, Plath was already a notable figure on the Smith College scene. She had graduated the year before and her poetry and 1953 suicide attempt were much talked about. When she returned to teach in 1957 with her husband, poet Ted Hughes, we were all in awe of the talented, glamorous couple. For some now-forgotten official reason—perhaps I was inviting her to speak at the Newman Club?—I went to interview her at their apartment. Surprisingly, I remember little about the meeting, other than that she seemed shy and diffident.

Today, I can appreciate our similar histories: two Smithies on scholarships, born a few years apart, with single mothers and "absent" fathers, sharing a racking depression that she, fueled by rage that was either too deep in me or perhaps not in my character, transformed into poetry. Some years later, my husband brought home a copy of *The Bell Jar*, which plunged me into a terrifying depression; it cut too close to the bone.

> **Journal entry, December 1990:** I had a hard time dig-
> ging out this morning. Perhaps it is an error to read
> Sylvia Plath's journals, which I bought yesterday
> and have read steadily since. I am a pale duplicate.
> She plunged into her demons early. In 1957–58
> when I must have met her, she was already intense-
> ly aware, had been hospitalized and indeed rescued
> from two suicide attempts. Her descriptions at 18
> are more knowing than anything I ever produced.
> At that point I was in a trance, and seemed to con-
> tinue in a painful dream state. . . . There was so
> much denial, repression, burial of feelings, unan-
> swered and unasked questions. I walked around
> in deeply padded armor which allowed only the
> intense scrutiny of others, never myself.

In the end, I was the luckier, I believe. I could not produce anything like Plath's sentences from *Letters Home*: *I am afraid of getting
older. I am afraid of getting married. Spare me from cooking three meals a
day—spare me from the relentless cage of routine and rote.* But I survived
to conquer my demons.

✦ ✦ ✦

In June of 1957, I met Neil—short for Cornelius—Bull, an "older
man" who taught at the Lawrenceville School, an elite prep school
in Lawrenceville, New Jersey. I'd been seated next to him at a
house party the previous Thanksgiving, but on that occasion he
was focused on another guest, Neal Blue, who had flown in a small
plane around Central America with his brother and was featured
in a *Life* magazine cover story.

Now, I was a bridesmaid and he an usher at the New Jersey
wedding of my college classmate Ginnie Teller—and this time
I was the object of his persistent attention. A popular master at

The weekend Neil proposed to me, June 1957

Lawrenceville, Neil had served two years in the Navy during World War II and then went on to Princeton University. At Lawrenceville, he taught history, coached wrestling, and managed the Skeet Club, along with being head of Cromwell House, a lower school dormitory. He'd been working there for nearly ten years and was now getting his master's in Latin American history at the University of Virginia.

The wedding was a three-day affair. Neil arranged to be seated next to me at each event and between events stayed close to my side. We caused a lot of speculation, and I was told years later that we had stolen the wedding. Romance, however, was far from my thoughts at that moment. My upcoming job in the offices of a flooring mill in Walpole, Massachusetts, held little interest and I was facing the prospect of an uneventful summer. I had an assortment of local boyfriends to go out with, but overall the school break loomed as an interruption to my absorbing life at Smith. In only one more year, I would have to face the mystery of what to do after graduation.

Everything changed for me over the course of that wedding weekend. Neil dramatically upped the ante by asking me to marry him on the second evening. Utterly dazzled by this charming man and totally unprepared for the impact of his proposal, which I did not respond to, I danced and socialized and tried to deny what was unfolding. He pressed to drive me home from New Jersey to Massachusetts.

"Mimi, are you in love?" My mother immediately sensed something in my voice when I called to arrange this plan with her.

"No, certainly not! I mean, I don't know!" I wailed.

Being very curious to meet the man who had so clearly unsettled her daughter, my mother agreed to meet us en route in Framingham, Massachusetts.

I don't remember much about that drive north with him other than asking him, as we crossed the George Washington Bridge, how old he was.

"Guess."

He did not correct to eleven my guess of "ten years older than me."

When he met my mother, they began a firm friendship that lasted until her death nearly thirty years later. I drove the rest of the way home with her, undoubtedly relating to her in detail the firestorm weekend I had just been through.

Back at home, the contrast of my quiet summer schedule in its

First weekend together in Martha's Vinyard, July 1957

humdrum world enfolded me. Impressions of that beautiful wedding weekend lingered like a dream. Its very unreality convinced me that I had awakened to a long, empty stretch until my return to college in the fall. The lack of immediate communication from Neil made me begin to assume that for him it had been a lark and that his long drive home to Charlottesville had given him time to reflect on his impulsiveness.

I began my job facing the practicality of earning money for the coming year. About ten days later, my mother called me at work to say there was a telegram from Neil that began *I want to be with you, in old Tashmoo*. . . . It was a bit of doggerel inviting me to Martha's Vineyard for the long Fourth of July weekend. Suddenly my gray summer burst into Technicolor, initiating a nearly fifty-year ride on the tail of the comet that was Neil Bull. We were not formally engaged until my Halloween birthday so that I might catch my breath. "I'll take you to all the places you dream of," he said. He more than kept that promise.

✦ ✦ ✦

We were married three days after my graduation in June of 1958. The Smith College commencement speaker that year was a handsome and promising young senator from Massachusetts named John F. Kennedy, who, at a time when women did not hold leadership positions in American society, urged us, as able and educated women, to consider politics as a career.

As she told my daughter, Holly, many years later, my mother, after graduation, went back to Norwood alone with little more than $20 left in her bank account.

We went off on our honeymoon. Neil's English relatives, the Aspreys, owned a hotel in Mandeville, Jamaica, "in the cool of

My wedding day, June 10, 1958

58

the hills," and they provided us with a cottage on Discovery Bay. Neil had been warned to limit our honeymoon to two weeks as we might run out of things to say! Having seen little of each other during our engagement, we really didn't know one another and that might have been true. But we began our lifelong delight in each other's company, exploring the island with similar curiosity and at a congenial pace that would characterize our well-traveled marriage.

Those two weeks in Jamaica set the tone for our next forty-six years together, which was marked by adventurous journeys, a conversation between us that did not stop, and encounters with interesting people. When I went for Sunday Mass, Neil hit it off with Father Benjamin Judah, the Jesuit priest in the little church in St. Anne's Town. Being of African and Jewish ancestry, Father Judah had needed several special dispensations to become a Jesuit. He was a passionate collector of cameras and other hobby equipment to fill his solitary existence. He had ordered the equipment for a skeet field and Neil, as the skeet coach at Lawrenceville, was a godsend to him. We spent hours getting Father Judah's skeet field set up, and later, over refreshments in his cottage, learning about the island.

The cottage staff included a gardener, a driver, and Alberta, the cook. Alberta amused us one evening when she took all the wedding rice that my bridesmaids had stuck into my luggage and added it to one of our meals.

Toward the end of our stay, we met a retired American impresario, Hal Peet, who lived nearby and invited us to extend our honeymoon by coming to live in his guest house for as long as we wished. However, Neil's mother had planned a party in Charlottesville to introduce me to her friends, so we had to leave. Though we didn't yet know it, the wedding rice did its job—we had a baby son on the way.

My mother-in-law, Helen Bull, known to all as Gee, would

prove to be a challenge for me. The only child of a wealthy New York Jewish couple, she'd spent much of her adolescence in Europe with her widowed mother and met Cornelius Bull II in England, where he was recuperating from his service in World War I. After having two children, they divorced. As a wealthy divorcee summering at Rehoboth Beach, Delaware, in 1929, she learned she had lost everything in the Crash. It's a testament to her character that she did not crumple, like her mother, under this blow, but went straight to work for the first time in her life. To make her living she opened her large, well-staffed Washington, DC, home to boarders—young officers and working women—and also ran the bookstore at the Shoreham Hotel. Though barely five feet tall, Gee was a lively and formidable presence. A veteran smoker and bourbon drinker, she loved to laugh, was always meticulously dressed, and hosted famous parties. Eventually, she became a real estate broker and later moved to Charlottesville, where she was living when I first met her.

Because of Neil's speed once he had resolved to marry me, she probably did not have time to voice her objections to the marriage. And objections there were, as I subsequently learned. I was neither socially prominent nor from a wealthy family. What's more, I was Polish, Catholic, and the daughter of a single woman who was a hairdresser. Gee had raised her son to move in privileged circles, and, to her mind, he was a remarkable catch. She held strong opinions about life's "shoulds" and "oughts," and her expectations were certainly dashed by his choice of me. Fortunately, I didn't realize the full extent of her initial disapproval, perhaps because Neil was firm in cautioning her to accept me, which in time she did.

LAWRENCEVILLE

We started our married life in a large apartment in Griswold House at the Lawrenceville School, where Neil was housemaster to forty-five boys. It was the first of many homes I would decorate to our own taste as we made our way, like foreign-service officers,

Griswold House, 1958

to various posts. At Lawrenceville I found myself pouring tea and coffee after dinner and making conversation with a smart, lively bunch of adolescent boys. I was not much older than they were, and it is just as well that I was not a mind reader! I cheered their house games and learned to provide what were termed "feeds." Whenever Neil spontaneously announced one of these treats, our apartment was immediately besieged by boys, who swept in to devour all the eggs, pancakes, chips, peanut butter, jelly, cookies, milk, orange juice, etc.—whatever we could find in the larder to temporarily appease their ravenous appetites.

Few of the faculty wives had full-time jobs in those days. I worked mornings in a nursery school where I had my first experiences with little children, until my own pregnancy made it difficult to bend over and deal with their elaborate snowsuits and tend to whatever else had to be done. I learned to give dinner parties using my wedding gifts: I set out small silver ashtrays at each place, and set cut crystal fingerbowls on lace doilies by each dinner guest after dessert and before the liqueurs were brought out. It

61

amazes me to remember doing that. These days the dessert, if there is one, goes into the fingerbowls, and the little ashtrays are long since packed away with the rest of the tarnishing silver.

Our son, named Neil after his father, was born in 1959 during spring vacation. Within a few days, the senior Neil flew to Reno to interview for a job as founding headmaster of a new independent school in Carson City, Nevada. My mother-in-law had provided me with a baby nurse named Mrs. Hankinsen ("Hanky"), an experienced and reassuring grandmotherly presence in my bewildered new motherhood. She was not, however, convinced that her little charge was getting enough sustenance from my nursing, which I wanted to do after Nelie's—as we called young Neil—natural childbirth. With improved anesthetics and regular formula, the practices of natural childbirth and breastfeeding had been out of fashion for decades. The headmaster's wife sniffed, and allowed that she had seen Italians on buses nursing their babies. So, it was an uphill battle.

Along with these minor obstacles, I was slowly sinking into postpartum depression, at the time an unrecognized issue of new motherhood. I was unable to talk about it, admit it, or know what was wrong with me, so there was nothing to do but ride it out. The luxury of stepping away or taking a break was not an option; I was under pressure to "be myself" again. But a lingering sense that something was wrong remained. My husband was busy every day, we had little time alone, and I sometimes felt isolated and desperate. Though I did make an array of wonderful friends during those two years in New Jersey, I was too ashamed to confide these dark moods to anyone. At some point, Neil pointedly told me about his Aunt Lib, and how she had made her husband's life miserable with her emotional ups and downs. I took the hint and henceforth was determined to keep my own counsel whenever the unexplained mood change overtook me.

Neil landed the job in Nevada, but as it turned out, there were

Me, Neil, and Nelie in Norwood, the day before Neil left for Turkey, 1960

insufficient funds to open the school. His appetite whetted for a headmaster post, he interviewed a few months later with Duncan Ballantine, president of Robert College in Istanbul, Turkey, and was hired to head up Robert Academy, a prep school for boys affiliated with the college.

Suddenly Neil now had to finish his work at Lawrenceville and complete his master's in history at the University of Virginia within the year. I would produce our second son, Sam, and plunge into the monumental job of preparing for three years in Istanbul by assembling and packing items as yet unavailable in Turkey from a long list of suggestions provided by Robert College's New York office. In the early 1960s, such items included a pasteurizer for the daily delivery of unregulated raw milk, a Maytag semi-automatic washing machine with wringers, a three-year supply of clothes for two growing toddlers, clothes for me, and extended household necessities including a large freezer I filled with boxes of Pablum and forty-eight rolls of toilet paper. (We discovered later that, after four to five months in transit, the Pablum tasted like the TP.) Instant coffee, Worcestershire sauce, and cloth diapers, along with some of our wedding presents, were also forwarded to make our house into a home ready for family life and extensive entertaining.

In the midst of all these preparations, fifteen-month-old Nelie came down with a persistent low temperature and barking cough. My pediatrician in Trenton sent us to Children's Hospital in Boston, where Nelie bounced and squealed with delight in his isolation chamber, cheering up the staff, who were used to children in more advanced and sadly debilitated condition. He was diagnosed with a rare but treatable form of tuberculosis, and the doctors put him on a protocol of pills that he would take four times daily for the next two to three years.

Nelie, once out of the hospital, and I stayed with my mother in Norwood in the final months of my pregnancy. The older Neil was away in Charlottesville, finishing his master's degree, and then he left for Istanbul in mid-August to take up his new job. I suffered the August heat of Norwood in those days before air conditioning, and still remember the suffocating sense of masking and robing myself (over the all-encompassing maternity clothes) before entering Nelie's isolation chamber in the hospital.

Sam was born in late September on the day of Nikita Khrushchev's famous shoe-banging episode at the United Nations. My mother and I listened to the debate on the radio as we awaited Sam's emergence in the doctor's room. I had chosen again to give birth without anesthesia, and the hospital staff marveled at Sam's alertness when he finally arrived.

My mother became increasingly distressed as the reality of my departure, and that of her grandchildren, began to set in. She had bonded closely with the babies, was fond of my husband, and had expected to be part of our lives as she had been in our past two years at Lawrenceville. She was anxious not only for what lay ahead for me but also that she would soon be left feeling very alone and very far away.

TURKEY

Air travel was still in its glamorous stage in 1960. One dressed well, and for my departure, a group of family and friends gathered with champagne and gifts and encouragement. It was a sendoff similar to what one might have expected in those early days sailing the Atlantic on a Cunard liner.

Not yet twenty-four, I was making this long trip alone with two young children, one of whose health was compromised, on the old Pan American Flight 1, which circled the globe in a westward direction. By now, the two-and-a-half-month separation from Neil had overtaxed my patience and I could think of little else but arriving in my new home and settling in with my family to start a new life. The people gathered at the airport in New York shared my mother's misgivings and concerns at my setting off into an unknown world. In those days, little was known of Turkey and the most recent news was of a *coup d'etat*, when the army took over the government of Adnan Menderes. Martial law prevailed, and had my mother known that there were heads hanging from the Galata Bridge when Neil arrived, she would have staged her own rebellion. I was oblivious to all of their concerns, aware only that I would soon be with Neil again and would be introducing him to his second son.

It is difficult to imagine how Pan Am could have arranged more torture for me on that trip. The glamour and service was for businessmen and stewardesses, not lactating mothers with babies. Crammed in the inner two window seats with one-month-old Sam in a crib attached to the bulkhead taking up our leg room, we were confined for the next fourteen hours. Next to me on the aisle for the first leg to London was a professor from Columbia University, hoping no doubt for a long, peaceful read. I apologized when the consistently unhelpful stewardess brought me a bottle for Sam that was far too hot and I was forced to nurse him, an act not performed in public in those days. In London, the break that had been promised to me, in which I could get off and stretch my legs and change out of the skirt stained with the coffee Nelie had spilt, never materialized. In Frankfurt, all passengers were ordered off the plane, and at that point I put my foot down and refused. I brooked no argument with my clueless stewardess and she went off to inform the pilot. But when he came back to enforce the ploy to get passengers into Frankfurt's newly opened duty-free shops, he took one look at me, with my hundred pounds of carry-on luggage and two little ones, and made an exception.

The last leg of the journey featured Aramco Oil Company families headed out to the oil fields of Saudi Arabia with lots of children, all seated with me in tourist class. Their mothers were delighted to let their children go and see the baby Sam. Exhausted and frantic by now with a sleepless Nelie, I did not welcome these little visitors. To cap things off, the crew ran out of food while serving from the rear forward, so by the time they got to us there was only the aroma of hot meals being served around us.

All those hours later, after leaving my mother and friends in New York and having experienced some of their apprehension, I looked down as we descended into Yesilkoy Airport at the edge of Istanbul on the Sea of Marmara. Neil had been promised a limousine by the director of the Istanbul Pan Am office to take us home in comfort. At least in those days before tight security restrictions, he could board the plane and help us off. A group of Robert College and Academy faculty were there, lined up on the tarmac bearing flowers to welcome me. Among them was Traugott Fuchs, who handed me a bouquet of *karanfil*, clove-scented carnations that gave me my first rich sensory experience of Turkey. Some visiting VIP had preempted the limo to complete the Pan Am fiasco, so we headed into the city in one of the more ancient of Istanbul's ancient fleet of taxis. It was Cumhurriyet Bayram, Turkey's independence day, and all the mosques in the city were illuminated, giving me a truly magical first view of the city I would come to know and love so dearly.

✦ ✦ ✦

The faculty members of both Robert Academy and Robert College, plus those of the neighboring Girls College, were an adventurous lot. To sign up, sight unseen, for three years of teaching in Turkey (which we would extend to six) was not for the faint-hearted. There were Americans, Brits, Russians, Poles, Germans, Swiss, Swedes, and the local Turkish faculty, among whom were Armenians, Greeks, and Jews. Before our departure, we had been told by a Lawrenceville colleague who had taught in Turkey, "Mimi, Neil, you are about to enter a fraternity of friends who will be friends for life." We had no idea then of the truth of his emotional declaration.

✦ ✦ ✦

Located seven miles north of Istanbul, Robert College (now Bosphorus University) sits on the hills above the Bosphorus on its European shore, overlooking the wide arc of Bebek Bay with its pleasure boats, seaside villas, restaurants, and shops. Istanbul's climate is rather like that of Washington, DC. In the spring the hills are covered with flowering Judas trees and lilac blossoms, and in June the fragrance of wisteria mixes with the incomparable song of the little brown nightingales that court ecstatically in the low, dense

Robert College, ca. 1961

shrubbery. The climate is tempered by winds from the Black Sea and the occasional *lodos*, a southwesterly wind said to bring physical and emotional malaise.

Below the college, rising on the narrowest section of the Bosphorus, sits the fortress of Rumeli Hisar, built by the Turks in the fifteenth century while they were laying siege to the capital of Byzantium, then called Constantinople. In the 1960s, the shores of the Bosphorus were still edged with the lovely wooden *yalıs*, or summer houses, where, in former times, wealthy Ottoman families spent the warmer months. When we arrived in 1960 there were no more than a million and a half people in Istanbul. The population has grown in the intervening years to upward of sixteen million. The bridges were not yet built that would lead to the heavy development of the then-quiet and pastoral Asian side of the Bosphorus.

Our two-story stucco house stood at the edge of the hilly Robert College campus. With its four bedrooms and bath around

Our home above the Bosphorus, 1960

Nelie, Rumeli Hisar, and the Bosphorus, 1961

a large upstairs central hall, and a living room, dining room, library, and kitchen around a downstairs entry hall, it became in time a charming and comfortable home.

Beyond our small walled garden unrolled a steep, bowl-like hillside, a natural amphitheater behind the fortress around which threaded a narrow path to several faculty houses and then down to the village of Rumeli Hisar. That path came around the bowl, through our garden and on up to the college, making casual drop-in visits a pleasant part of my days. The doorbell rang often. In addition to friends, there were twice-daily deliveries from the Bebek market, along with the *sütçü* (milkman), the *muzcu* (banana man), the man who sold innards, and now and again a knife sharpener. The *eskici*, the man who bought junk and whose call our children loved to imitate, was a periodic visitor, and at various seasons, gypsies came by selling mistletoe or mushrooms. Sometimes a tambourine signaled the arrival of a gypsy with a chained bear who danced for coins. One memorable sight was my garbage collector, or *çöpçü*, sitting on a trash can poring over a discarded *Princeton Alumni Weekly*. My busy husband once asked me what I did all day. I replied, "I answer the door."

One day shortly after I arrived, Neil announced to me, a novice cook and hostess, that he had invited twenty-four guests for a formal Christmas dinner, and then left me to get on with it. And six weeks later—during which time I also settled into a new house, managed two babies, negotiated the shopping in an unfamiliar language, struggled with a primitive kitchen and a sweet but incompetent maid my well-intentioned husband had hired— the appointed time arrived. With the tables set and decorated and the food and babies under control, I suddenly realized I had to dress. I stapled a long piece of Thai silk to a black waistband and topped it off with a silk blouse. On the menu: roasted goose with browned southern rice, red cabbage, and trimmings, topped off by a flaming plum pudding proudly brought in by our giant Tatar gatekeeper, wearing a crown of bay leaves I had gathered from the hedge by our house. The evening was a grand success. I had met my husband's challenge, a fact I still marvel at. And there were many more dinners to follow.

+ + +

For my mother, at this point, I might as well have landed on the moon. Skype and email were a half century in the future, and I'd boarded that Pan Am flight knowing I would not see her again for three years. Telephone service at that distance was erratic and expensive. So I wrote her detailed letters, all of which she kept. They describe the daily novelty of my life in Turkey, our travels, and the progress and activities of her grandsons.

As I reread her letters, I wonder how I could have been so unaware of her loneliness. A lot had happened to me in the two and a half years since my wedding. There was hardly time to integrate my own experience of marriage, motherhood, the male world of

Lawrenceville, and now this life on an exotic perch at the edge of Asia, never mind grasp what *her* experience was. We lived together in those letters.

✦ ✦ ✦

I was an eyewitness to an event that has entered Robert College lore. One morning, as I walked up the path from our house to the campus, I found a large dump truck parked in the lot above our garden. A strong odor came at me as I realized the mammoth gray mound on the truck was the carcass of an elephant, its inert trunk dangling over the side. My husband arrived to tell me that Lee Gardner, the biology teacher, had heard the elephant had died in the Istanbul Zoo and had immediately hatched a lesson plan for his unsuspecting students. They would dissect the elephant and then assemble the bones as an exhibit for the college's small natural history museum. Maggots were needed to clean the dissected bones and had to be ordered from the States, post haste.

Lee didn't factor in the sluggish Turkish Customs office, and the maggots arrived as dead as the elephant they were meant to devour. Eventually both maggots and elephant had to be disposed of—but where? Alumni still come to me and claim they were dumped into the Bosphorus or buried in one or another of the faculty gardens.

The same Lee Gardner called me one day and asked if I would take in three orphaned brown bears. Their mother had been shot in the Ataturk Forest and he, of course, immediately planned a zoo for his students. I couldn't resist and that afternoon, a sturdy, waist-high cardboard packing box was delivered to my kitchen. Inside were the bear triplets with their eyes still closed, a delectable sight. Lee provided a small, nippled bottle and some vague clues as to their feeding, and left me to get on with it. I worked out a system of feeding them individually. Before they woke, I took one cub, fed it, and placed it elsewhere to enjoy its sleepy fullness. I

Holly and the three bears

then fed the other two in turn so that as they grew more lively I wouldn't have to deal with their insistent squalling. At the end of the process, I would take the three in my lap and give them each a finger to suck on. Soon I'd have a lapful of purring cubs, roaring their content. If my doorbell rang often before, it rarely stopped now as news of the cubs spread. To manage this disturbance, I made a batch of vodka and mixed up several large apothecary jars of Bloody Marys and invited the community for an afternoon reception to meet my bears. They were a great hit and some semblance of peace was restored to my house.

One evening in the spring of 1966, we were heading out with a small party for dinner on the Bosphorus. I was dressed and ready but still finishing up the bear-feeding routine. I was sitting on the floor of the kitchen with the three bears in my lap purring away when one of the dinner guests, the writer James Baldwin, appeared. As he stood framed in the kitchen doorway, his great eyes doubled in size as he took in the sight of his hostess on the floor feeding her cubs. We relished Baldwin's presence in the Robert College community when he spent time in Istanbul. The Turks did not recognize him, so he was free to wander the streets with his friends without being approached, as he was in other cities. His secretary, David Leeming, chaired the Academy English Department, so our students benefited when he spoke eloquently to them about literature. In a letter to my mother, I wrote:

> We talked [with Baldwin] about a great many things that evening. He was particularly interesting on the subject of Truman Capote and his latest novel-reportage, In Cold Blood. He spoke of his friends, both famous and unknown, Marlon Brando, James Jones, Bill Styron. He was warm, responsive, and disarming, and as he became slightly liquored we got to the inevitable subject of integration. I have never talked directly and at length on the subject with a Negro and certainly never with one so articulate. For the first time, I peered into the depths of their feelings. My God. His language became raw, brutal, and charged with the awesome road ahead. I asked him about these projects to take ghetto boy and girls and put them into schools like Exeter or Princeton. I couldn't pin him down here because he was partly teasing me but really he doesn't think much of this. He sees no progress until the basic economic structure of the country is changed. This is massive and will mean a lot of battling and strife before we get there, if indeed we ever do.

✦ ✦ ✦

In the year before his death, while his cancer was in remission, my husband said: "I never worked a day in my life." He relished his profession, worked very hard, and was popular and successful as a young headmaster, appreciated and beloved by the Turks. In our 1950s-style marriage, I supported his career and raised our children. Securely established in a family with a position to uphold, I had the thrill of seeing, for what I assumed then was the first time, my own flesh and blood in my children. I was rooted in a firmer soil than the quicksand story of my childhood. I was happily married and loved the adventure of our life together. And yet, in those six years abroad, I was periodically beset with enervating low moods that I could not account for. The *lodos*, that unnerving wind from the southwest, had me in its sights.

After Neil came home one day in the company of Warrick and Helen Tompkins, a couple he had met walking on the Robert College campus, I began to understand my problem. They came for lunch and stayed on with us for three days. Helen was a psychotherapist; before they left, she asked if she could speak to us in her professional capacity. She said she had observed that I was *depressed*, that it was sapping my energy. She urged me to seek professional help. It was an enormous relief for me to hear that. Under assault from depression, I had to fight at times to entertain, to be a good mother, or simply to leave the house. With no understanding of what was going on, I had been extremely hard on myself.

Psychotherapy was still in its infancy then. Mental illness was deemed shameful, something to be hidden. Neil was unable to accept or cope with this condition of mine, and we had to decide if we would put our limited funds into treatment. Nevertheless, he wanted the problem fixed, and so I made an appointment with a Turkish psychiatrist. After I described my presenting condition— happily married, mother of three, absorbed in my life as headmaster's wife, yet periodically laid low by dark moods—he suggested

Me at Rhodes, 1961: a life of exotic travel underlaid by dark depression

I go home and decide if I wanted to work with him. I never went back. At the time, I thought seeing the psychiatrist wouldn't be worth the expense. Now, I believe it would have been a waste, as the critical information about my identity would not begin to emerge for another dozen years.

During a trip to Rhodes in 1961, I was terrified by my first suicidal impulse—a genuine desire to throw myself off a steep hill as we climbed to see an ancient ruin. As a practicing Catholic, I was in part restrained by the enormity of the sin of suicide. And I could not fail or disappoint my husband nor devastate my mother. Most of all, it was impossible to leave my children. I moved to a new level of desperation. What was wrong? And why, when I was leading a life I loved, did this cloud keep reappearing?

In the face of this puzzling debility in his normally intrepid and cheerful partner, my husband felt uncharacteristic helplessness that turned to anger. In response, I strained to hide my depression

Florence and Gee with Nelie, ca. 1960

from him. I was like the duck in
the old Turkish saying, calm on
the surface but paddling like hell
underneath. More ashamed and
isolated than ever, I lay awake at
night weeping in desperation at
my situation. Helen Tompkins
had said that depression makes
its victim expend ten times the
usual energy, and it was true for
me. I became subject to chronic
bronchitis, which put me in bed
periodically with legitimate and
defensible cause.

Art Therapy Drawing No. 2.
A self-portrait. Depression in the
mid-section, the ball and chain of
secrets, a stapled mouth.

+ + +

Our daughter, Holly, was born in 1962 during one of the worst
winters in memory. We lost our dog to starving wolves that came
to the edges of the city. The *Paris Tribune* reported people in England digging potatoes with drills. I'd had in September what our
doctor felt was whooping cough and landed in the American Hospital, where there was room for me only in the men's ward. So
intense was my coughing that I feared that, like a scene from an
Egyptian myth, my baby would be born through my mouth. But
Holly arrived in the normal way on a snowy Christmas morning,
conveniently timed so that my husband and his mother could leave
me for a friend's holiday party. Gee, who was on an extended visit,
had hoped to get home before this birth. She did not approve of
my housekeeping and parenting, and was convinced of my un-
fitness to be a headmaster's wife. More inclined to judge than to
help, she managed to escape in early January. Three-day-old Holly
spent her first night out on the town sleeping in a basket at Abdul-
lah's—a posh restaurant once filled with spies and diplomats and

renowned for its scenes of international intrigue—as Neil and I joyously celebrated her arrival.

Holly was baptized in the tiny local church in Bebek, which was tucked up in a corner of the village and presided over by an ancient Bulgarian priest who seemed not to be fluent in any familiar language. When we married, Neil, an Episcopalian in name only, agreed (as the Catholic Church required) that our children would be raised Catholic, and in the early years of our marriage I was a weekly attendant at Sunday Mass. In the Lawrenceville years, I went to the Princeton University chapel to hear the firebrand Hugh Halton speak and to mingle with the interesting community that he had attracted. In Turkey, the children and I were part of a congregation that included a small group of émigrés and a few local remnants of a dwindling Catholic community. An array of Russian, American, and Turkish friends welcomed Holly to her spiritual life.

+ + +

A couple of months before Holly's birth, my mother wrote to confirm that Jack Whelan had proposed to her and that they would be married in the coming year. I was delighted. I remembered Jack, a dentist with an office adjacent to my mother's beauty shop, as a quiet man who kept to himself. Rather than my returning to the States for the wedding, she wanted to come and visit the world I had described at length in my letters, spend some time with her grandchildren, and purchase a wedding ring.

After Father Hip's death six years earlier, she had returned to an empty house and her job in the beauty shop with few expectations for any change in her life. What with graduation from Smith, marriage, adjusting to the world of the boys' prep school, and the arrival of my first child, I had been too absorbed with the abundance of change in my life to recognize the depth of her loneliness. Now, as she was looking forward to marriage and becoming a member of Jack's large family, she relished the prospect of her first trip abroad and seeing her grandchildren again. By seeing where I lived, she would be able to better visualize my life in the years to come as I described events and the progress of the children.

Florence arrived to a joyful reunion with her daughter and grandsons. In her quest for a wedding ring, Neil and I took her to the Covered Bazaar, to the inner sanctum of the Zincirli Han, a quiet courtyard filled with carpet, jewelry, and antique shops, plus a noted dealer in ancient coins, all of which Neil and I visited regularly. Centuries before, the *han* had been built as a caravan stop with rooms above for merchants and stables below for the animals. In the center of the sunny, open cobbled courtyard was a vine-laden well head and a small table where a rotating group of men bent over an ongoing, lively game of backgammon.

That afternoon, we took my mother to see Mr. Akaoui. Lebanese by birth, he had been raised in Beirut and Monte Carlo, where his family owned elegant shops. He had studied for some years to be an orthodox priest, but then had a change of heart. He was by now a long-married family man and an established merchant; his shop in the Zincirli Han catered to collectors of antique Ottoman and tribal carpets. He also carried a choice collection of antique jewelry. Not long before, he had proudly shown us some recently purchased jewels from the estate of Faruk, the late king of Egypt.

My mother, still lovely and always responsive to attention, fell under Mr. Akaoui's spell. As she looked over his collection, her interest was captured by a Russian wedding ring that featured a rare almond-shaped, peach-hued diamond surrounded by small rubies and mine-cut diamonds in platinum on a wide rose gold band. The game was on! He knew at once she would buy it, but the pleasure of the bargaining process was to be prolonged, savored, and brought to a conclusion that was memorable and satisfactory to both. Neil and I, sitting to the side, were spectators, as the spotlight was on the two of them. Both were at the top of their game and they played it out as it was meant to be. That long-ago afternoon in the bazaar springs to life now when I see the ring on my daughter, the heir to her grandmother's charm. My mother's happiness at her upcoming wedding was evident. The years of loneliness since Pate's death were coming to an end, and the marriage would at last provide her with a solid and more conventional position in her Norwood community, something I would reflect on and begin to understand only many years later, after her death.

+ + +

In a letter to my mother dated December 27, 1965, I described my last formal Christmas dinner in Turkey, an annual affair I had been preparing for faculty and friends since our first year at Robert Academy. The only difference this year was that it was a black-tie affair and people went all out in their preparations. The highlight was the group of men who had gone to the theater wardrobe and found nineteenth-century officer's uniforms with epaulets, brass buttons, braid, medals, and ruffled shirts. They lent a bit of magic to the whole evening. The festivities ended with the singing of carols and the playing of Dylan Thomas's recording of "A Child's Christmas in Wales." But the memorable part of that Christmas began the following morning, Christmas Eve, when, as I wrote:

> I hurried off to town to do my Christmas shopping. I was determined to find Neil a Turkish fireman's helmet, and the search for this item was an experience in itself. I had been told vaguely where to look but after wandering around fruitlessly in central Istanbul, I decided to go to the biggest fire station in town and ask—and I did that. You must

Sam (left) and Nelie modeling the brass fire helmet

realize what an odd thing this was to them in order to appreciate the story. No one here would dream of buying a fire helmet, let alone as a present for one's husband.

I marched into the large garden courtyard where there was a kind of guard house and a guard wearing just the helmet I wanted: a red helmet with brass decoration and a flap in the back to keep off the water. A magnificent affair and very dashing on these men with their great mustaches. He called out and wondered what I wanted and I pointed to his hat and said I wanted one like it. He was so flabbergasted that he could only grunt at his superior who was walking not far away. Now this man was a youngish man of the typical, often caricatured Turk: shaved head, great mustache, and very martial in his fireman's uniform. He wasn't about to be bothered with this strange woman who had invaded the masculine stronghold, but when I began to tell him what I wanted and he began to believe that I was serious, why then he became downright fascinated and almost smiled. Of course, by now a curious peripheral group had gathered and were edging around as close as they dared to find out what I wanted and yet still appear employed in folding hose (they had just returned from a fire). I asked them to write down the address he had mentioned and in a state of indecision my bald, mustachioed friend by this time was in conference with an amiable colleague and it emerged that I was to be given one of the firemen as an escort and we were to walk across town to fetch my precious hat! I left amidst all the elaborate Turkish goodbyes, thank yous and holiday greetings for my Christmas and their new year.

In the course of our journey through the iron mongers district, through muddy cobbled streets jammed with horse carts and *hamals* with their great burdens on their backs, I learned all about my escort's family. By great coincidence, he lives in an area which I am to visit on Monday with a Turkish woman pediatrician who is doing a pilot project on children's health in the Istanbul shanty towns. Of his seven children only three have survived and he hopes to be able to bring them to my friend during her free clinic hours. So, in all, it was a rather unique Christmas shopping expedition.

I went on to the bookseller's street and spent an hour with a charming Greek lady and bought some etchings for Neil depicting life in Ottoman Turkey. From there I went to see Mr. Koenka, the antique dealer with the great goiter, who sends you his Christmas greetings and says you must come back again. There I met Peter Shiras and we went for tea in a wonderful old place rather like our little lunch restaurant and we talked and talked about how nice our party had been.

That evening we went off with the Shirases to a special Mass at the Dutch chapel, the non-denominational chapel here in Istanbul. The chaplain there had assembled for this service representatives of eight different faiths to read the lessons from the Old and New Testaments concerning the coming and birth of Christ: a Capuchin monk representing the Catholic Church; Father Bissag Hatapian of the Armenian Orthodox patriarchate; Col. Lyman Barger, Methodist, Chaplain to the US Air Force; Father Gabriel, Greek Orthodox, Archimandrite, very high ranking like the Armenian above; Haralambos Melides, Minister of the Greek Protestant Church; the Rev. Helmut Tacke, Evangelical, Pastor of the German church in Istanbul; J. E. A. Bazalgette, Anglican, Secretary of the World Council of Churches; and the Rev. Melvin Wittler of the United Church. It was a very thrilling and deeply moving service that concluded with the lighting of candles in the darkened church, candles held by every person there, and then we filed out singing "Joy to the World" and gathered in the outer courtyard where we sang "Silent Night" and wished one another Merry Christmas and dispersed throughout the city to our homes. Everybody there felt that something quite extraordinary had happened to them.

And then Christmas morning. The children found their stockings upstairs and we were awakened to the ecstatic squeals of delight for the stockings were filled with pencils and small toys and flashlights and Nelie even broke out in a yell over a tangerine that he found in the toe. They received clown outfits and books and tops and Nelie, a musical instrument called a Melodica. At one point, he draped his clown suit over his back and lifted his arms—*I'm the man in church,* he announced. He was playing priest. I nearly split myself laughing.

Neil overwhelmed me with a jewelry box that he had made from an old microscope box with brass fittings. In it I found a lovely necklace and a receipt for a set of the OED, a dream come true after I first found it in the Smith College library. . . . He loved his hat and the Ottoman prints which I think I mentioned.

So now it is Monday morning and I am relaxed and spent. It is a luxury to see a blank calendar ahead of me. Neil leaves on Wednesday for Rome and Paris and will be in the States until New Year. I am sending Özcan [the maid] off for five days and being able to settle down in utter peace with the children will be bliss.

At this sitting it looks very likely that Neil will find a job and that we will be home this summer. I live these days with a constant lump in my throat and glue my eyes to all the places that I love so dearly—to make an indelible impression.

✦ ✦ ✦

I marvel now at our good fortune and privilege at having spent six years in Istanbul—it has deeply enriched my life in some way nearly every day since. We lived a charmed existence. Orhan Pamuk describes that time period in *Istanbul: Memories of a City*, but our Istanbul was not infused with his *hüzün*, or melancholy. The depths of gloom that intermittently encased me stemmed from a past I neither knew nor understood; it was not endemic to Istanbul, which we saw with the eyes of adventurers.

We were young and filled with curiosity and surrounded by a cohort of similarly adventurous faculty and friends. We explored the city with Godfrey Goodwin, an authority on Ottoman architecture, and travel writer John Freeley, who led us on weekly tours through all the extant Byzantine churches and ruined palaces, through the Ottoman mosques and palaces, the hidden *hans*, the city hostels for caravans, and the back streets for traces of all the different stages of Istanbul's rich and complex past. In addition, we spent many weekends with our friend Bob Hardy, an intrepid collector of Russian silver, Chinese export porcelain, Kurdish aprons, carved wooden coffee boxes, and, above all, beautiful carpets. A University of Chicago-trained Hittite scholar, he had also been a World War II code breaker. In Bob's company we became regular visitors at the Covered Bazaar, where we were shown the latest rare carpets, textiles, porcelain, or jewels that our favorite merchants—Jak, Lutfi, Monsieur Akaoui—might have acquired since our last visit. As they grew older, the children were free to roam at will in the bazaar, playing their invented games in the mazes of inner courtyards and passages. All of their developing senses were challenged in these swarming surroundings as they absorbed the dense variety of visual riches, colors, textures, and smells.

Perhaps the most important thing I learned from the Turks was their staunch and deep commitment to friendship and how to practice it. My childhood in a quiet household with its potent secrets was not conducive to the art of friendship. Our circle was restricted to my mother's family, her customers, and few others. People were drawn to her, and for her many customers she was a discreet and compassionate receptacle of problems and sorrows. But entertaining and easy back-and-forth among friends was not a notable part of my upbringing.

The Turks quickly changed all that. On my arrival at Robert College, after overseeing the chores of settling into our new home and then producing a Christmas feast, I'd begun to consider what we might do as a family for our first Christmas in Turkey. I managed to round up some presents and we found a small tree to decorate, imagining that it would be just the four of us. But late on Christmas morning the doorbell rang. Standing outside was Mithat Alam, one of Neil's Academy students, together with his sister and their parents, laden with beautifully wrapped packages.

"We came to wish you a Merry Christmas as you are spending this holiday so far away from your families and friends," they told us. "We will be your Turkish family while you are here."

I am as moved now, sixty years later, as I was that morning by these words. We were taken into the Alams' circle, and though Mithat and his parents are gone now, many of his friends remain our friends to this day. The Turks have a generous-spirited and whole-hearted commitment to friendship. When they emigrate, I believe they suffer less from homesickness and more from "friendsickness."

SEDONA

We had lived in Turkey for six years. Many American and other foreign families remained for their careers at Robert College, but we made the difficult decision to return to the States. The children, aged three, five, and seven, were at a stage when it was easy to move them into American schools, and so Neil accepted a job at the coed Verde Valley School in Sedona, Arizona. It could hardly have offered a greater contrast to Istanbul. In the high desert,

Verde Valley School, late 1960s

a hundred miles north of Phoenix, the school was located in the heart of dramatic red rock country, offering Grand Canyon landscape on a human scale.

We moved in the summer of 1966 to a campus of informal adobe and wooden buildings set among giant cottonwood trees that form an oasis amid the sage and juniper landscape that encompassed mesas and rock formations familiar to fans of western films. At an altitude of 4,500 feet, Sedona provided the ideal climate for clearing the respiratory and bronchial problems I'd experienced in Istanbul. I flourished, as did everyone who lived there. Whey-faced teenagers metamorphosed into young gods in that dry, sun-drenched high country. The red, powdery dust of Sedona permeated everything. Years later, I opened an antique brass lantern clock to show its workings to a friend, and out poured a familiar stream of the fine, red powder.

We continued, young Neil and Sam and Holly and I, our practice as Catholics, attending the dramatically situated Chapel of the Holy Cross. The pastor was Father William McNamara, a Carmel-

Father William with Holly seated behind

ite monk who had been chaplain to the nuns at my high school in Brookline, Massachusetts. His was a rollicking, celebratory Mass with the overflow of children seated on the altar steps, rocking to live contemporary folk music and quieted by Father William's sermons, which he delivered in his deeply resonant, Irish-inflected voice. With the blessing of Pope John XXIII, he was in the early stages of establishing the Spiritual Life Institute, a community of Carmelite monks and nuns. It was the beginning of a friendship that lasted until Father William's death in 2015.

✦ ✦ ✦

The children settled in with a pack of faculty kids and went to school in Cottonwood, a long bus ride each day. At home on the Verde Valley campus, they roamed the high desert landscape and swam in the creek. We were too remote for television reception, so as in Turkey, they read and played and were out of doors. One memorable day when the boys were seven and five, I was pressed to the limit by a trustees' lunch at our small house, followed by a dinner in the evening for faculty and trustees. After the lunch, I had to dash to town for groceries. I left the two boys and made them swear they would not leave the house until I returned. I made the twenty-five mile round trip in good time and went in to face the chore of cleaning up the lunch dishes and launching into dinner preparation—only to find that the boys had, like the shoemaker's elves, magically done all the cleaning up. I sat before them and wept in relief at their initiative.

If I thought in the early weeks that we had landed at the end of the world, I was soon to discover otherwise. The student body was drawn from an array of families of writers, anthropologists, architects, and a large contingent from the Hollywood film industry. Surprise was the order of the day. I answered a knock at a side door to my house one day to find an infuriated Burt Lancaster, lost on a walk while his daughter was being interviewed for admission. Or the day when two construction workers nearly fell off a building when they looked down to see me in the company of actor Robert Wagner. Another day I walked into the reception area outside my husband's office to find him and another faculty member in a helpless state, with tears of laughter tracking paths down their cheeks from the non-stop stories of Walter Matthau, who was waiting while his son spoke with an admissions officer. Jack Lemmon's son and two of Burgess Meredith's children also came. One day, driving around Sedona doing errands, I had a genial passing flirtation with a bearded fellow in an antique green Buick. When I returned home I found that unmistakable car parked in my driveway. There in the courtyard was the same man, now dressed in a white linen robe, sitting in meditation among my flowers. It was Ram Dass, who'd come to visit a student at the school.

One year Buckminster Fuller was lined up to give the commencement speech. Neil, who had often heard Fuller speak in Princeton, became concerned about his proclivity for long discourses extending to three hours or more. He called Fuller's assistant, who reassured him, saying, "Mr. Bull, as you lead him to the podium, simply say 'forty-five minutes, Mr. Fuller.'" It worked exactly as she suggested, and in forty-five minutes Fuller concluded to a long standing ovation. So, he proceeded to speak some more. One rarely hears of an encore to a commencement address. As I walked him back to our guest house, he asked if he might speak to the faculty in the afternoon after the students had left campus. Neil spread the word and everyone came to our house at 4:30 to hear more. At 7, I called the Owl Restaurant to ask if they could accommodate thirty-five to forty people on short notice, which they were happy to do, and Mr. Fuller spoke without interruption until 10:30 in the evening.

+ + +

My need for recognition, for being seen as a person in my own right, separate from my husband, came to the fore in those years. Intermittently beset with depression, I sometimes felt that if I passed a mirror, my image would not be there. But at the same time, encounters with the many guests who related to me not as a mother nor as a headmaster's wife, but as an individual to talk with and exchange ideas with, gave me some foothold on my sense of self. As a performer needs the next audience and applause, I needed the significant encounter, the recognition that I was truly there. I began to work at the school in several capacities and joined the board of Father McNamara's Spiritual Life Institute.

The construction of a new headmaster's house offered another creative and independent outlet that led to the discovery of the pleasures of gardening and, oddly, to the music of Gustav Mahler, a composer who would figure prominently when we moved later to Austria. I had recently bought Bernstein's recording of *Des Knaben Wunderhorn* in Phoenix (because of its attractive cover, I confess) and decided one afternoon to listen to it as I stained a set of tall, Spanish double doors. I nearly fell off the ladder as I heard the opening bars. With its dramatic beauty and exhilaration mixed together with the periodic assaults of unexplained somberness, I was hooked; his music perfectly suited the tone of my Sedona life. I built my Mahler collection and soon spent the occasional evening while my family slept listening to his music while smoking a black, gold-tipped Sobranyi cigarette from a pack left by a guest.

+ + +

My husband knew of my depression, but hiding it was by now my deeply engrained habit. I spoke to no one about it. I was adept at forcing myself to meet obligations and retreat when I could. Feeling helpless in the face of these on-and-off lapses in his wife, my husband, an activist, impatient to solve the problem, would resort to lectures about getting exercise or would storm around making order, picking up things that I was too weary to notice during these spells. Neither of us knew how to deal with my depression or why it came on. Though he was easy-going, charming, and wonderful company at most times, Neil was stymied by this problem that he couldn't fix. And that made him feel uncharacteristically helpless and probably trapped. I was driven further into despair. Propped by Slavic Yankee grit, I would reemerge from a bout of low spirits as my usually able self and we would move on. With good counsel at that time we might have avoided a lot of grief. I have spoken about my depression to lifelong friends who were astonished to learn about it—a tribute to my fiendish talent for hiding it. Had I broken down then or later, it likely would have benefited us all. I was breaking away from a pattern of so many women of my '50s generation who were trained in compliance to be caregivers and to feel a lot of guilt in every direction. My situation carried an overlay of conditioning: not to feel, not to question, and not to confide. And my marriage, while very companionable, was increasingly without physical and emotional intimacy.

+ + +

PRINCETON

Neil was increasingly at odds with his board of trustees, and his contract was terminated at the end of our fourth year in Arizona. Because of the politics involved on such a small, isolated campus, I was not unhappy to move on. We decided to move back to New Jersey to ponder our next step.

I flew to Princeton in early May to find housing, settle schooling for the children, and find a job for myself. Neil would work at the Independent Educational Services, a company located in downtown Princeton that he'd helped establish with his friend Bill Baeckler. In less than a week I found a book-lined Victorian house to rent while its owners were on sabbatical. With that settled, the children's schools fell into place, leaving me free from my heretofore seven-day-a-week job as headmaster's wife. I could begin to develop a resume of my own.

While in Princeton I was invited to a dinner party by my Smith college roommate and close friend Connie Moench Goodman. In addition to two of her husband's engineer colleagues who were visiting from Switzerland, she had invited her former boss, George Kennan, and his wife, Annelise. Kennan, a retired diplomat, had been one of the architects of Truman's Marshall Plan and served as ambassador to Russia and Yugoslavia. His writings had inspired the policy of containment. He was now a historian at the Institute of Advanced Study, an independent post-doctoral research center, where he was on the roster of well-known permanent scholars.

The evening was over too soon; there wasn't nearly enough time to say everything the good food and talk stimulated. I was left to hold my own with Connie and the Kennans while her husband, Al, caught up with his Swiss colleagues. Later, after saying good night to the other guests, Connie said to me, "You know, Mr. Kennan may be looking for a research assistant for next year. Write to him."

I returned to Sedona and my interest in such a position was further heightened by my husband's enthusiastic reaction to this unique job prospect. Though anxious and uncertain about my ability to fill such a position, I sent off my letter proposing myself for the job. A week later Neil walked up to the house with a small blue envelope addressed in a fine, slanted hand. The return address was Hodge Road, Princeton. Neil stood impatiently waiting for me to open it, while I, heart pounding, wanted to hold on to the anticipation. I was also preparing myself to face a polite and courtly rejection. I still have that letter. It was the herald of a wonderful thirty-plus-year friendship with George that began when I reported for work at Hodge Road in August of 1970.

+ + +

As I approached my thirty-fourth birthday that October, life presented me with bewildering and exciting changes that ushered in a period of decisions, of expansion, of opportunity. It was a time of revelations, of significant meetings and leave-takings, a year in which I met two of the most important male mentors in my life and a woman who would, by her example and her persistent prodding, awaken me from my 1950s' mindset, who would challenge me to search within myself for a creative outlet. It was the year in which my mother rocked me to the core with a startling confession, and, for the first time, I questioned our fifteen-year marriage; we were growing apart emotionally. It was a year in which I began separating myself from the Church and, for the first time, having doubts about my indomitable husband. And it was a year when I fell deeply in love.

+ + +

Here I circle back to the dramatic moment that opens my story—and, in fact, was the first step in opening my understanding of who I am. My mother and I, driving through the New Jersey countryside: she turns to me and says, "Mimi, I am your real mother." With that one sentence, she extends a branch of her family tree and I take it, one-half of my secret past now securely linked to Florence, to Alice and her sisters, to the Polish matriarch Paulina Czarnecki.

Who was my father?

She refuses to say.

From college on I had searched for father figures. I loved Fathers' Weekend at Smith, when my classmates' fathers would arrive. A friend and her father would adopt me for the weekend activities, and suddenly I was in a sea of wonderful proud fathers, steeped in a rich brew I had not tasted before. I would marry an older man, I would find both priestly figures and older men as mentors and repeat the pattern of close but not quite available men.

✦ ✦ ✦

My job with George Kennan was one of the life-changing events of that year. I arrived at his house at 9 each morning and went to his study in the tower room, where there was a wood stove and desk and an old couch, to get the day's assignment. He was in the process of writing the second volume of his memoirs, and so, in the first weeks, he sent me to the Princeton archives to read in his private papers—including childhood poems, early letters, and diaries—and thus familiarize myself with his younger self and his inner world, revealed in writings characterized by frank self-observation and self-criticism, with insightful descriptions of people and places rendered with a novelist's eye. I began to comprehend his deep sensitivity, his passion for literature, and his surprisingly wicked sense of humor. I was given the chance to look beyond the public figure, to the young boy who lost his mother early in life, to the awkward Midwestern outsider at Princeton, the fledgling diplomat, to the young husband and father taking his first steps on a path that eventually led to a distinguished and brilliant public career.

As time went on, the morning sessions with George became more relaxed, interspersed with his memories of Russian politicians or his recitation, by heart, of a beloved Pushkin poem in flawless Russian so I could hear the beauty of the language. Once he fetched his guitar to play some favorite songs. Often he would be reminded of funny moments in the formal diplomatic scene. One such scene had taken place during a dinner he attended in a crumbling, once elegant embassy in the Balkans. As the dinner was being cleared in preparation for dessert, the table suddenly collapsed in the middle. Servants were summoned and instructed to get under the table on their hands and knees and support it with their backs for the duration of the festivity. And if that weren't enough, while the embarrassed hostess struggled to regain her dignity, the butler whispered in her ear that in the confusion the dessert had burned and was completely inedible.

I had not yet begun to think of myself as a writer and would not take the thought seriously for another quarter of a century. But this apprenticeship with a fine writer opened a creative stream that I would begin to experiment with in the years to come: in my letters from Vienna in the late '70s and in journals I began keeping in the '80s. As I sat with Kennan, most memorably as he crafted a critique of Kruschev's memoirs for the *New York Review of Books*, I could almost see the material I had researched coming together with his remarkable memory and fed through his typewriter to emerge as lucid, elegant prose. His strict commitment and sense of responsibility to the truth was an example I have not forgotten, especially now as I see the ravaging effects of "fake news."

✦ ✦ ✦

During Columbus Day weekend I took the train from Princeton to Boston to visit my mother. I've traveled that route since I made my first trip to New York when I was six. After making my way through a half dozen cars, I took the only seat available on the busy, student-filled train. It was a holiday weekend and, in that era before everyone disappeared into phones or laptops, the car was filled with excited conversation. After talking with some of the students, I turned to my seatmate—a tall, slender black man, graying at the temples and wearing a clerical collar—and noticed that he was absorbed in Germaine Greer's newly published *The Female Eunuch*. I was struck by the sight of a minister deep in a book about feminine empowerment and so, catching his eye, I asked, "What is a distinguished man of the cloth doing reading *that* book?" My directness startled him and his slow smile evolved into a deep, rich chuckle. And we proceeded to dive effortlessly into an intense conversation that lasted until I staggered off the train outside of Boston five hours later. My mother was there to pick me up and, ever-observant, asked, "Mimi, what has happened to you?" I was far too dazed to give her a coherent explanation.

It is impossible to reconstruct the content of that conversation. What I *can* say about it is best expressed by Herman Hesse in his novel *Demian*: *One never reaches home, but where paths that have affinity for each other intersect, the whole world looks like home, for a time*. For two people of such utterly different cultures and backgrounds—he, a black Protestant minister, two decades my senior; I, a white, New England Catholic woman with her first job—we discovered, to our mutual astonishment, common ground within seconds of our meeting and, in the ensuing few hours, laid the foundation for a thirty-five-year relationship, one marked by an intimacy and trust that always allowed us to find home in each other's company—and conducted primarily by telephone and mail and a rare meeting in person.

Ben became friend, mentor, lover, and father figure. I was able to meet his formidable intellect with feminine perspective, as a challenge, as muse, and as someone to whom he could freely confide his triumphs, sorrows, and frustrations. In return, I had someone who cherished me in ways that nourished my emergence and who filled needs I hardly knew existed. That we managed our deep connection over the next three-and-a-half decades was miraculous. We had rigid boundaries to keep, and to violate, in order to create a safe time and place for us to meet, outside of our lives, while at the same time protecting our families. As a known figure in his world he could not compromise his standing—there was never a question of that—nor was I at all inclined to change my situation. An open friendship was, naturally, out of the question, for both of us, and thus I found myself, once again, in a vital, yet necessarily *sub rosa*, secret relationship. And I was terrified, as he certainly must have been, of our being discovered. *I can't do this*, I said to myself, knowing simultaneously that I couldn't *not* do it, that it was a matter of my emotional survival. I know now, in retrospect, that turning away from him at that critical juncture would have meant the real loss of a healing connection, a closing down that might have turned me into a lesser and bitter human being. And if I *had* said no, I'm sure that my ever-vigilant guardian angels would have arranged another momentous train ride to challenge me.

+ + +

Fate, in her lavish abundance, sent into my life that year these two remarkable men: Kennan and the man who, to protect his privacy, I am calling "Ben." Though they met me in different arenas of my life, both encouraged and supported me and challenged me to grow; both were convinced that I was up for the challenge. With my mother's remarkable revelation, I would benefit from their commitment to me as I reconfigured my life story. Their recognition and support were crucial as I began to think about what I would do with my life as my children were growing up. They would both remain an important part of my life until their deaths.

+ + +

My friend Ernestine Ruben, whom I met that year, was well launched into the professional world of photography. From the onset of our friendship, she has probed and nudged and challenged me, demanding that I express myself. With her successful forty-year career as an artist and teacher, she has served as my model of a single-minded, committed, late-blooming artist.

+ + +

Our brief year in Princeton was truly a life-changing period for me and a time of reassessment for my husband after the unhappy conclusion to our stay in Arizona. My mother's surprising disclosure amounted to a radical readjustment of my life story, and though it anchored me in reality with a degree of truth I had never known, it also raised many new questions.

James Baldwin wrote: *We turn to each other in the hope of being created.* From my long experience with invisibility, with not being a "realgirl," I think that what Baldwin refers to—the power of re-creation that exists between people—comes in large part from the way one sees and is seen, from acts of *witnessing*. On the professional level, my year in Princeton presented me with new and challenging work, which, to my surprise, I completed successfully. Kennan's undisguised admiration and satisfaction with my work made Neil stop and take notice of me in a new way. The meeting on the Amtrak train brought Ben into my life—a person who *saw* me as I wished to be seen. I stepped fully into adulthood that year; I chose my own work and no longer took all of my cues from my husband's agenda. And because I could step back, I was able to see with a new objectivity that my choice of partner—the purely instinctive choice of a twenty-year-old girl—had been a sound one. And Neil, as he wrestled with a profession setback, was newly vulnerable and found that he needed his family and needed me.

The family and Gee, Neil's mother, spring 1971

VIENNA

Neil and I were both eager to live abroad again, and in the summer of 1971 we moved the family back to Europe. We flew to Paris, rented a car, and then drove on to Vienna. Neil had accepted the job of headmaster at AIS, the American International School, located in the suburb of Salmannsdorf on the northwest edge of the city, within walking distance of the Vienna Woods. We were there for five years.

The comfortable headmaster's apartment, with plenty of room for a family of five, was located on campus on the top floor of a large pre–World War I villa that had been built by a Viennese banker as a summer house for his extended family. The first two floors were, in those days, the offices and classrooms of the middle school. From the long terrace that ran the length of the top floor we had a fine view of the distant city, and at night we could admire the small candles burning on the gravestones of the cemetery on the opposite hillside. On the morning of our arrival, as we were moving our luggage upstairs, we noticed a large, heraldic shield hanging on the staircase landing. On it, printed in the old German alphabet, was a rhyming inscription that began *In Salmannsdorf, so wird gesagt* . . . It declared that Salmannsdorf ("Suleiman's village") had been named for Suleiman "the Conqueror," the Ottoman emperor whose troops had camped on this spot during the sixteenth-century siege of Vienna. It concluded by stating emphatically that Suleiman had *not* succeeded in taking the city. We were pleased by this reminder of our happy years in Turkey and took it as a good omen.

After the transitional year in Princeton, the children thrived at AIS. Their teachers were excellent, they made friends from all over the world, and the safety of the city in those years and its excellent transportation system meant they could, if they wished, move about on their own. Young Neil spent his weekends at the open flea market, collecting old tin boxes, keys, canes, and whatever oddities his allowance would allow. He later joined the English Theater to indulge his growing interest in acting. Holly would march down the hill to a sweet shop to spend her allowance, and Sam busily collected things for his protracted trading sessions with Neil. Neil, despite being the oldest, had chosen the smallest bedroom and set up the first of his hermit scholar lairs. Sam, less interested in décor, took the largest room. Always organized, his desk drawers were labeled "Miscellaneous Stuff," "More Stuff," and "Other Stuff." Holly had a beautiful room, its walls stenciled in blue, with an alcove containing a built-in wash basin. Tidy and organized, she always knew exactly where everything was.

Reading my letters to my mother from this time, I observe how our stint in Vienna, more than any other segment of our life, provided a social and glamorous time filled with entertaining, travel, and a great deal of music and opera. But I liked Vienna so much less than Istanbul that, for many years, I put it aside in my memory. I found it difficult to revert to my position as headmaster's wife after the challenge and independence of my job with Kennan. I inquired at the American Embassy about taking the Foreign Service exam and was stunned to discover that, at thirty-five, I was too old to apply. For a while I worked the Theater an der Wien with Marlus Melkus, the set and costume designer for children's productions. I also started the first of a series of small, informal women's groups that I would either initiate or join in the years to come. We gathered to visit exhibits and to take day trips in and around the city.

Skiing is very popular in Austria, so much so that the schools close in February for a ski week holiday. We had several good ski trips during our stay in Vienna, but the first one, to Villach in southern Austria, was the most memorable, for all the wrong reasons. The children, all well-coordinated athletes, went into a ski school where the instructors did not realize they were beginners. That, combined with bad ski bindings and terrible snow conditions, brought two of them down with broken legs on our very first day out. I rode the cable car down to the hospital with Sam, who had broken one leg, and was met there by my husband, who brought Holly down twenty minutes later with two broken legs. Because the hospital staff could not calm Holly, who continued to shriek after her bones were set, I called the orthopedist, Dr. Otto Russe, at the Vienna Hospital. He suggested I hire an ambulance and get them to his hospital, where he would meet us. This was arranged and, still in my ski clothes, I climbed in with the kids and headed north for the five-hour trip. Sam had books to read and settled in, but Holly continued to howl non-stop. As we passed through towns on the way north, the ambulance drivers, unnerved by her distress, would say, "Madame, there is a hospital here, should we take her to it?" "No," I would answer, "drive on." With just an hour left to go we ran into blizzard conditions on the

Semmering, a mountain on the Vienna outskirts. The drivers lost their way, adding drama and exhaustion and yet another hour to the trip. Finally, after 11 at night, we reached the hospital and, true to his word, Dr. Russe was there to greet us. Within minutes Holly was finally given some relief, and both children settled in a room to sleep. I asked if I might stay with them as by now it was midnight. I was in an unsafe part of the city, and what's more, I realized, I didn't have the keys to our house. "Madame," the doctor said, "we are not running a hotel." With ski week under way, all of the faculty families were out of town. I didn't think to call our friends, the Humeses, the American ambassador and his wife, and finally remembered Shifra and Jerry Rosen, a couple we had only recently met. They agreed to put me up for the night; it was a sudden and surprising beginning to a long friendship. Jerry, fluent in German, stepped in to manage the situation and soon the children were set up at home with two hospital beds, side by side to make it easier for me to care for them—and for them to bicker endlessly. Neil, having brought young Neil, the dog, and our things back from the ski resort, promptly left for America to recruit faculty. As Sam and Holly recuperated, their legs began itching inside the plaster casts—and they made their discomfort known! Gerd Schleimer, the business manager at the school and a veteran of the partisan wars in Yugoslavia, came to visit and silenced their endless complaining with a war story. He gave them a graphic description of what it was like when lice got into dressed wounds or inside casts. He left two uncharacteristically subdued kids behind when he departed.

Other trips were more successful. We all loved Venice so much that we returned there for nearly every Easter break during our time in Vienna. It was an overnight drive away, and the *pensione* we returned to year after year welcomed our dog, Daisy.

Our trip to Greece in the summer of 1974 was also memorable. Through our friends Magali Gaster and Hilmar Gottesthal, an Austrian painter, we rented (for $14 a month!) a little house in the coastal village of Stomion, not far from Larissa. We had two rooms, a kitchen, and a central hall opening to a balcony that overlooked a small walled yard with a well, an outhouse, and the hen house. Magali and Hilmar were well-known in the village and so we got to know some of their friends, particularly two young men named Thanassis and Yorgo. Yorgo had recently been injured in a bad fishing accident and was known ever after as Cut Leg Yorgo to distinguish him from all the other Yorgos in the village. We didn't learn Thanassis's nickname until the last day of our vacation. Young bachelors, these two attached themselves to us, sometimes dropping in at Magali's for a drink or cavorting with the children on the beach. Thanassis got his arresting looks from his mother. Lean and browned by the sun from her job cleaning the beach each morning, Yahya, as we called her, had close-set blue eyes and a pronounced nose. She wanted her youngest, Thanassis, safely married and settled down, but his escapades kept her head continuously shaking in dismay. He was having too much fun with the influx of bikinied tourists from Yugoslavia and Poland. In repose, his face was dour, but his smile or laughter made him irresistible. He sailed each winter with the Greek merchant marine and had been able to buy a house in Stomion. At the end of the summer, I went to say goodbye to Magali who had, she told me, just recently learned Thanassis's nickname: "The Flyer." She poured me some *tsiparo*, the local version of ouzo, and told me the story.

In midlife, her other children grown, Yahya had a fling with a stranger, forgot about it, and then, several months later, accompanied her friends on their annual expedition to Mount Ossa, where they gathered branches of the linden tree so they could make the blossoms into a medicinal tea. Yahya had climbed up into a tree to break off some of the higher branches and then had no time to get down before Thanassis made his entrance into the world, swinging in mid-air at the end of his umbilical cord. Considered a kind of miracle, he was viewed by the villagers as an angelic presence whom they ever after called Thanassis the Flyer.

Some three or four years later, after we had moved away from Vienna, we were sitting down to dinner in San Antonio, Texas, when the phone rang. I went to answer it and a deep, gravelly voice on the line said, "Allo Maria? This is Thanassis. I am in Greek bar in Houston. Come and dance with me!"

✦ ✦ ✦

Still wanting work, I went in answer to an ad to a job interview with Victor Gruen, a retired architect, city planner, and environmentalist. His American publisher had asked him to write his memoirs and he needed help to get this project under way. A Viennese Jew by birth, he had left Vienna in 1938 before Hitler marched in. Victor arrived in New York City with $13. With the help of other immigrant Austrians, he found work at the 1939 World's Fair pavilion and soon began designing store fronts. He eventually founded an architectural firm that built the first US shopping centers. The environmental impact of these large shopping enclaves led to his interest in city and environmental planning. He had recently returned from the States to live in Vienna with his fourth wife, Kemija.

It was she who greeted me at the door of their apartment. Behind her I could hear an irascible voice: "I don't want to see anyone. They won't do. Send her away!"

"But Victor, she has come all this way. You must see her for a few minutes at least."

"I don't want to. You talk with her!"

Kemija, undaunted, looked at me and said, "We'll go. Victor, we are coming in!" At a large antique table slouched a small man in his seventies. He had lidded eyes behind large tortoiseshell eyeglasses and he continued to protest until we were introduced.

Kemija knew her man; she knew he could not resist a few minutes with a good-looking woman.

"All right," he relented.

I reassured him that my husband and children were waiting outside in the car and that I would not stay long. We began the interview and, two hours later, I begged off to rejoin my family.

Thus began one of my more unusual jobs, a comic unfolding of an unproductive but, for me, absorbing view into his world-spanning business. Unproductive because he was still brimming with ideas for the future and was resisting looking back and putting a period to his long career. Instead, Victor, a gifted raconteur, preferred to puff away at his cigar and fill our hours together with stories of pre–World War II Vienna, when his father was a lawyer for theater and opera figures, and descriptions of the world of the Viennese cabaret, the setting for brilliant social and political satire.

✦ ✦ ✦

I'd become connected to the English Chapel, an enclave of foreign residents drawn by Prelat Ungar, who often said Mass there. Urbane, witty, and worldly, he had been director of Caritas, an international Catholic charity, and, I believe, had lived for a while in the US. I remember him asking me, with a wry smile, why American toilet paper and Wonder Bread were indistinguishable.

Our children were in early adolescence by now and I was starting to wonder why I was hauling them off to church each Sunday. Through these years, my intermittent bouts of depression and occasional thoughts of suicide were checked not only by the love of my family but also by the strict teachings of the Church on the subject. But my faith was waning and at some point in those five years in Vienna, my irregular attendance at Mass stopped altogether. I remember listening instead to the Sunday morning Vienna Philharmonic concerts broadcast live from the Musikverein. Leaving behind the lifetime habit of church-going was like a gradual climate change. I didn't consider joining another church either then or later, but I continued to read widely about soul and spirit and people's experience with the beauty of the transcendent. I had the basic teaching and culture of the Catholic Church in me; I needed no more doctrine. My retreat from the Church had no emotional connection with my father, as I was still ignorant of his identity. I simply slipped into a kind of inactive and remote Catholicism. I never departed from the core teachings of love and compassion that Catholicism shares with all the major religions. What I *did* reject was the body of regulations and teachings of a misguided patriarchy that has lost its way and stubbornly refuses to face the skeletons in its closet. I had no clue then that these would become very personal issues for me later in life.

At the same time, my mother was feeling a similar estrangement. She had continued to attend Mass and receive the sacraments, but had become disillusioned with her experience of uninspired churchgoing, devoid of any spiritual teaching or compelling leadership. Her husband, Jack, felt the same way. Disenchanted with the stale experience, they stopped going altogether.

+ + +

As intriguing as my two jobs had proven to be, I needed to begin to add to my resume and earn some money. Neil recognized this and began looking for work in the US. We had been in Vienna for five years, the children were on the brink of college, and I would need to work to help finance this next stage of their lives and find a satisfying challenge for myself.

San Antonio, Texas, 1976

SAN ANTONIO

In 1976, we moved to San Antonio, Texas. My husband became headmaster of St. Mary's Hall, which, at the time, was a girls' K–12 day and boarding school on a lovely campus designed by O'Neil Ford, an architect who had recently been named a National Historic Landmark by the National Council on the Arts, the only individual to ever be so designated. A friend sent me a clipping about this and, on a whim, I sent Ford a note saying that I could not write to the Alamo, the other San Antonio national treasure. I told him I admired his work and that I had partially fashioned our Sedona house on photographs of one of his designs. I mailed the letter and forgot about it.

In our preliminary interviews with the school trustees, I had informed them that I could not be a traditional headmaster's wife, that with our boys nearly ready to enter college, I would need to find full-time employment. With their contacts and influence, I soon had three excellent possibilities: as assistant to the president of the newly established University of Texas at San Antonio; a similar position with the Institute of Texan Cultures; or as a program administrator with the university's Continuing Education Division, which had offices on San Antonio's famous Riverwalk. The job with Continuing Education was the first one available, and so I met with its director, Sandra Cook, a fearsomely bright, imaginative administrator. She was drawn to the diversity of my life, to my work with both Kennan and Gruen, and to the fact that I had no experience in, and therefore no preconceptions about, continuing education. She was a remarkable person to work for; she put her trust in me and let me go. She gave excellent advice and firm support when needed, and nudged me beyond what I thought I could do. I thrived. The job gave me carte blanche to approach and employ interesting people in town or elsewhere—writers, artists, professors, museum and zoo directors—to conduct short programs for the adults of San Antonio. For example, I drew on my Turkish experience to invite Douglas Tushingham from Toronto to do a three-evening program on the Iranian Crown Jewels, a collection that he had evaluated and documented for the shah, and Dennis Dodds, director of the Textile Museum in DC, who flew in to do a series on Middle Eastern rugs and textiles.

One day, some months after our arrival in San Antonio, I answered the phone and heard a man's voice saying, "Mrs. Bull? This is Neil Ford. Your charming letter came to cheer me when I was recuperating from a heart attack and feeling old and depressed. Please may I take you to lunch and make up for my delay in answering you?"

I took him up on the invitation, of course, and after lunch, he took me along the Riverwalk, which he had designed and behind which he was the driving force. Any walk or collaboration with this captivating person was an anecdote-filled, laughter-drenched adventure. He went on to do several programs for me on historic preservation. They sold out because he was a beloved figure in San Antonio and a very engaging speaker.

This job was all mine. I relished its possibilities and created programs that were copied around the country. One was called "Behind the Scenes at the San Antonio Zoo." The zoo director introduced the students to the practical issues of zoo management and led them through the kitchens, the nursery, and the infirmary. We had to run that program over and over as word spread and people from around south Texas came to participate.

My working life became the source of our social life, and that too was a big change. Neil was happy to see me absorbed and challenged and our savings for the children's college fund began to increase. It was a tremendous boost to my sense of self, of self-worth, of achievement. Working flat out both at the university and entertaining as headmaster's wife, I seldom had any bouts of depression.

Jerry and Shifra Rosen, the couple we had met in Vienna, were set to join us in San Antonio. Neil's hiring of new faculty was sometimes too controversial for the San Antonio board of trustees, particularly in the case of Jerry, as the generous terms of his contract raised some eyebrows. This led, in part, to Neil's eventual dismissal. That was ironic in the long run, because Jerry's creative combination of administrative and fundraising abilities and his long tenure served the school brilliantly and moved it to a new level of excellence.

Before we left San Antonio, I was offered a position at Trinity University, establishing a national speakers program, but it never occurred to me that I might stay on in Texas and take the job. I was soon headed back to Princeton, New Jersey, with my family to look for a home and a new job.

PRINCETON, AGAIN

Having purchased a stucco house with three apartments located just minutes from the center of Princeton, we loaded up a truck with our belongings and drove across the country, caravan-style, in August of 1978. Young Neil was headed to Cornell, Sam had finished Texas Military Institute and would be heading off a year later to Princeton University, and Holly would finish high school at Princeton High School, located just minutes away from our new home.

With some solid experience, a fatter resume, and the need to work, I headed to the Princeton University employment office. The staff there liked my resume but, having no openings, referred me on to Educational Testing Service (ETS), located just outside town. A few days later, I started work in their department of Educational Services under the benign and courtly direction of James Dineen, a former Jesuit. My first assignment was to put together a conference for headmasters and board chairmen for which I drew on my twenty-five years of closely observing private schools. It was a great success, and I was selected to join a small team putting together the Arts Recognition and Talent Search (ARTS), a program to recognize American high school seniors gifted in dance, music, theater, visual arts, and writing. No one believed we could pull it off, but, under the meticulous direction of the formidable program manager, we did it.

The best part about creating the ARTS program—the aspect that offset all of the administrative headaches—was the fun of working alongside the experts we hired to review the applications and select the finalists. I worked with both the dance and music panels, whose members included Charles Reinhart, director of the American Dance Festival, Karel Shook, co-founder of the Dance Theater of Harlem, Walter Nicks, a noted New York dance teacher, pianist Claudette Sorel, who arrived every day with a Mary

Poppins-like bag of sweets and goodies to press upon us, and William Warfield, the opera singer who sang "Ol' Man River" in the film version of *Showboat*.

This experience led to a friendship with Charles Reinhart that continues to this day and, through him, to becoming a board member of the ADF, a post that took me to the organization's summer residency at Duke University in North Carolina for many years.

+ + +

The challenge, variety, and pace of my work at ETS kept my melancholy at bay, but did not heal it. With my mother's revelation, my back story had changed from being an adopted child of two women to a secret, illegitimate child with an unknown father. It was something new to dissect with the array of psychiatrists and counselors I consulted, who were as clueless as I about the source of my malaise and unable to help with my nameless confusion in the midst of a diverse and interesting outer life. Onc program, however, did prove useful. During our ten-year stay in Princeton, I discovered Ira Progoff's Intensive Journal seminars and participated in two of them. They introduced me to a systematic and comprehensive approach to the exploration of one's self, emotions, history, spiritual life, family relationships, friends, lovers, work colleagues, and public figures, both alive and historical. I stumbled into a kind of writing—Ira's systematic journaling that encouraged inner dialogue with significant aspects of one's life— that would play a critical part in helping me to make sense of my self and my world.

PART THREE

*Holding on to secret material may be
translated by the child as a need to hold back.
Thus one cannot move forward in one's life until the
secret is shared, or the burden of secrecy lessened.*

—THOMAS COTTLE, *Children's Secrets*

I N MAY OF 1983, my mother and her cousin Lidia invited me to accompany them on a trip to England to visit relatives in Leicester. I had recently quit my job with ETS, and I accepted. We spent a few days in Leicester and it all—atmosphere, rhythms, Polish faces—seemed very familiar to me. But, at my mother's request, I was still keeping up the masquerade of being her adopted daughter, so I felt like more of an observer than a participant. When we returned to London it became clear that, while valiantly trying to keep up with Lidia and me, my mother was not well. She was too tired in the evenings to go with us to supper or performances. I found a Turkish restaurant near our hotel, where Lidia and I feasted in the warmth of the owner's hospitality, and returned to my mother with delicious foods he sent along to tempt her indifferent appetite.

Shortly after our return to the States, I was back in Paris with my husband. We had had a wonderful time walking the West Highland Way in Scotland several years before and were now intent on another walking adventure in England. Before we could go anywhere, an urgent call from Jack summoned me home. My mother had been diagnosed with stage four colon cancer.

Discouraged with her doctors' lack of commitment and indifference, she felt desolate, isolated, and weak. My arrival cheered her and, with improved spirits, she began to eat and gather strength. I called our friend Hilary Koprowski, a noted biochemist affiliated with the Fox Chase Cancer Center. He fielded questions about my mother's prognosis and told me that he and colleagues were involved in research on monoclonal antibodies and would be willing to include her in the study. Could I bring her to Philadelphia in September for a series of experimental treatments? I quickly agreed. Florence was still well enough to travel and it would be a chance for us to have her stay with us and spend time with her grandchildren.

In light of the situation, my husband insisted that we tell our by now college-aged children that Florence was, indeed, my mother. After initial resistance, she agreed. The result was unexpected for all of us. The children saw her in a new light. She was truly their grandmother—their own flesh, a novelty for them in our small family. This surprise truth released a flood of affection for her, something she had long craved, and for those weeks she was strong enough to be the funny, fun-loving person I remembered from my days growing up in Norwood. She regaled them with stories about life with me, and seemed relaxed and happy for the first time in a long, long time.

Her reception into the program at the Fox Chase Cancer Center was red-carpet all the way, and she responded to it. She found herself among many others living with cancer and it gave her more perspective. Because it was an experimental protocol, she felt her participation was important. Whether it worked or not—in her case, not—she felt she had contributed something to science. Coming to Princeton blessed her in two ways: being part of the study gave her a sense of purpose, and she had shared a remarkable time with her grandchildren. In the last days she was with us in Princeton, I took her into New York City to shop at Saks, to see a Broadway musical, and have a last glimpse of the city she had always loved—and where, I would learn later, she had once spent two weeks with my father, vacationing together like a "regular" couple.

In the following months, as her condition worsened, I drove up to Norwood every couple of weeks to be with her. We began to go through her things, telling stories, remembering our life together, and finding my letters interleaved in the books and magazines that filled the house. When the weather and her strength permitted, I'd take her for an outing to her favorite café.

✦ ✦ ✦

While all this was going on, my two younger children had become interested in an Indian guru named Babaji of Herakhan.

Holly and Sam had been introduced to Babaji and his teachings by a friend from San Antonio who was at Princeton with Sam, and were making plans to travel to India in November and asked me to come along. Stories of charlatan gurus were much in the news at the time, and so I agreed to go; I was determined to see this teacher and his community for myself. The intrepid traveler in me also loved the idea of going up the headwaters of the Ganges into the Himalayan foothills. My mother was ill, and yet my maternal red alert was strongly urging me to fly to the other side of the world. I decided to go. My mother understood this and encouraged my choice.

✦ ✦ ✦

I arrived at Delhi Airport in the middle of the night. Following the instructions in the *Small Planet Guide* and taking care not to awaken the many sleeping bodies on the ground, I made my way to the British Veterans' Bus Service stop. A very clean bus with only one other passenger—young, cheerful, and memorably foul-mouthed—dropped me right in front of my hotel, where I found Holly in her room with a high fever. Her first. The hotel staff called a doctor, who gave her antibiotics and instructed her to sleep, which she did while I went out to explore the city on my own. When she was well enough, we took an eight-hour bus ride north to Haldwani, where we checked in at the designated guest house to await an invitation from Babaji. Said invitation in hand, we continued on the last leg of the journey to his ashram, on foot, up the river with guides and pack mules to carry our luggage.

On arrival, we were shown to the women's quarters, a long barracks-like room with bars on the windows to keep out monkeys and leopards. Cots were crowded side by side along opposite walls. Lit only by candles, with laundry hanging along the middle, the place was a fire trap, basically. We settled in, adjusted to the one-meal-a-day schedule of subjee, a vegetable stew at midday, bathing in the river, and, with no outhouse, relieving ourselves wherever we could. Above us, farther up the hill, were Babaji's quarters, a gathering courtyard for evening puja and chanting, and, off to its left, the quarters for his long-term devotees. Sam was housed there and would stay on and travel with Babaji after Holly and I eventually left.

I found a very well-heeled group of people there from Italy, Switzerland, France, Israel, and America. Since I was menstruating, I was not allowed into Babaji's presence—which was perhaps for the best as I was in fierce mother-protector mode. I wasn't worried about Sam, but I didn't like the idea of Holly as one of Babaji's acolytes. My plan was to wait her out—which gave me time to absorb the beautiful riverside setting among the steep, jungle-covered hills. Across the shallow river, the Babaji group had built an enclave of small temples. I am grateful to have been there while Holly weighed whether she would stay on or not. I took a page from my mother's parenting example and said nothing, but waited until she was ready to leave. Sam stayed on for several months, traveling with Babaji through Gujarat. He benefited from his experience in India and has returned often.

Holly and I went on to Agra, where we sat together at the Taj Mahal for an entire day, seeing it in all kinds of light and watching people from all over India in richly colored regional dress coming to pay homage. We also went to Jaipur and then met my husband in Kathmandu at Christmas. There, I met Tibetan refugees for the first time and began my commitment to their cause, later going to the Carlyle Hotel in New York City to meet the Dalai Lama. I had read Fosco Maraini's *Secret Tibet* years before in my mother-in-law's library, and that led me to read as much as I could about Tibet's culture and religion, as well as many early travel accounts of those who had penetrated into that mysterious land. When I went to the Tibetan temple in Kathmandu, my tentative arrival was greeted with offered tea and encouragement to enter and be welcomed to a room full of cheerful young boys and lamas chanting.

+ + +

After my return from India, I began a schedule of spending two weeks with my mother in Norwood followed by two weeks at home in Princeton. In May, I wrote in my journal:

> She seems better as the time approaches for me to be there—but that could be my imagination. As things change in her condition—pain, sleepless-ness, discomforts—she is reluctant to seek help and Jack is not assertive either. So I go in and ad-just and make the changes or arrange for the assis-tance needed. She seems to give up between my visits. As my arrival is imminent, she is picking up again. I can improve her food, entertain her mind, reminisce, gossip, chat about my life, the kids, whatever. It puts her in touch again. The phone doesn't do it in the same way. I am getting more emotional at odd moments. Ben made the com-ment that I mustn't adjust too much or too well. It worries him that I seemed too well for what I was going through.

I learned a lot about her delight in food. It irked her terribly that food now seemed so dull. I saw also how sadly she felt the loss of her looks. She had always taken pleasure in her appearance. I wondered what I was avoiding, what more should be faced, talked about. My conditioning as a child was to not ask questions, but now I was wondering about what I would want to ask her when it was too late. With nearly grown children, I needed to know who my father was, what our heritage, ethnic background, and health history might be. And I felt those questions somehow held the answer to my periods of depression, my sense of being other, being apart, not belonging at some basic level. I never said these things to her. When I asked about my father she avoided the issue, sometimes saying she forgot. But now that she was clearly failing, I hoped she would not die and leave me missing this vital piece of my identity.

In her final months, my mother was too weak to stay up past dinner. I spent the evenings with her husband, Jack. I had known him and some of his children since I was in elementary school. Quiet, slim, unassuming, he did not socialize with the other tenants in the building that housed his dental office and my mother's beauty shop. His first wife had died of cancer, and I felt sorry that he faced this ordeal yet again with my mother. Some years after his first wife's death, having been left with five nearly grown children, three still at home, he'd began to court my mother. They were married while we were living in Turkey; she moved into his house and began to make a home for his kids. In his despair, bewildered about how to manage his teenagers, he'd started drinking to excess. Jack told me later that she had saved his life.

She opened his world by making a home that was comfortable and welcoming to his friends and to his children. She brought him to visit us in Sedona and later to Vienna, on his first trips away from the Boston area. She learned to play golf to share his favorite activity, and encouraged his interest in music. In those evenings, while she slept upstairs, he talked about how he'd wanted to be a jazz musician as a young man, but that after returning from the war, he had taken up dentistry as a way of supporting his growing family. He was a good dentist, but it was not the work he dreamed of. He and my mother shared this reality of being locked in jobs they did not love. He talked with me in a way that amazed his family when I happened to mention these conversations.

As I went through my mother's things, I continued to find, and re-read, the letters I had written to her through the years. I

Florence and Jack, late 1960s

reviewed my own life as I watched my mother's close down. Her renewals of energy upon my arrival soon became less and less animated. I stayed on now, as she was completely confined to her bedroom. She had struggled to be up, to not be a trouble and not have to be waited on, but her energy was flagging. I had brought her music on a tape recorder—her opera, her Chopin, her Marian McPartland—but she no longer had the energy to listen. Instead, I sat with her, to be there when she wakened.

Sitting with her in her final hours gave me one last chance to broach the crucial subject of my paternity, but, even at this stage, I was still fighting my lifelong habit of not questioning her. She was lucid but clearly succumbing to cancer. I took a deep breath and asked her—no, I begged her—to tell me who my father was. She gazed at me for what seemed a timeless moment . . . and then slowly turned her head away, as inscrutable now as she had been all her life. After this, her final refusal, I felt empty and defeated.

It seemed I would never know the answer. She had revealed to me what was, I imagined, her most shameful secret: having an illegitimate child. Why, then, was she unwilling, or unable, to tell me my father's identity? Was she bound by some promise to him? I would soon learn that others knew Father Hip was my father. Why could she not bring herself to tell me?

+ + +

Florence's funeral reception was held in September 1984 at the Whelan house on Rosemary Street. The last guests to leave that afternoon were Lidia and Adeline, two of her cousins, whom I had known all my life. Lidia, at 74, was my mother's age; Adeline, nearing 60, was closer in age to my 48 years. Both women were unmarried and had lived at home with their mothers. I had never been free to discuss with either of them the fact that Florence was my birth mother.

With her death, I could now ask them, "Did you know that she was my real mother?"

Adeline, the family gossip, jumped in. "Oh yes, of course we knew, but we never talked about it out of consideration for her."

Emboldened by this, I asked, "Well, do you have any idea who my father was?"

A look of pure disbelief flitted across Adeline's face, and I realized at once that not only did she know his identity, but she was astonished that I did *not* know. Standing in the light rain near their car, I was also aware of how uncomfortable this conversation was making Lidia, who was more the naïve maiden aunt than Adeline. In truth, I was not ready to have Adeline tell me right then. After the intensely emotional events of the day, the certainty that I would at last learn about my father was more than enough for me to absorb at that moment. But at the same time, feeling drained after all the emotions of my mother's final weeks and my despair at her refusal to reveal my father's identity, a tide of relief was pouring through my system at the thought that I was, at last, getting close to knowing this major piece of my story.

After they drove off, I went back inside. Jack was upstairs resting, exhausted by the day's events. My husband was packing to drive home to New Jersey, and all I could tell him was that Adeline knew who my father was, and that I would know soon. My plan was to stay on in Norwood for a few days to help Jack settle my mother's affairs. Neil departed soon after, and I was left alone to review the day as I finished clearing the remains of the gathering we had hosted for family and friends. I knew most of the guests from my childhood days in Norwood, but had not often seen them in recent years because of the peripatetic and diverse life of my adulthood.

The doorbell interrupted my reflections. My mother's close friend, Harriet Smith, was standing outside. She had been unable to face the funeral service or the crowd at the reception, and had told me that she would come to see me afterwards. I took her to the kitchen table and, over a glass of wine, we comforted one another and reminisced about her long friendship with my mother. Florence had seen Harriet through her divorce many years earlier and both had been single working mothers—still fairly unusual for women in the 1940s and '50s. Harriet had known me from early childhood and knew of my mother's pride in my family and in the travels that had taken us around the world. She also sympathized with the loneliness that Florence had experienced during the long years of our physical separation. She envied the closeness that Florence and I had shared, despite the distances, an intimacy that was a stark contrast with her bitter estrangement from her own daughter. Eventually, I broached the topic that was uppermost in my thoughts.

"Harriet, were you aware that Florence was my real mother?"

"Well, of course I knew. Many people knew, but no one ever talked about it. Everyone loved your mother."

The one and only photo of the three of us together

"Harriet, do you know who my father was?"

She looked shocked, as profoundly amazed as Adeline had been that I did not know the answer to this most basic of questions. She hid her face in her hands. "Oh, Mimi, please don't make me be the one to tell you!"

Not wanting to press, but urgently needing to know, I asked: "Did I know him?"

"Yes," she said, hardly able to breathe.

And then I knew.

"Father Hip?"

A pause.

"Yes."

+ + +

Ten years before, Harriet and Florence had visited me in Sedona, Arizona, where Harriet had seen Father Hip's picture in my living room. She had assumed that I knew he was my father. It must not have been a subject my mother discussed with her. Harriet knew I had spent the year after my mother's cancer diagnosis commuting between Princeton and Norwood, helping Jack and spending time with Florence as her health worsened.

Harriet departed and I was left in the silence as Jack slept on upstairs. I was swept with a deep feeling of peace and serenity at the rightness and logic of this revelation. For a second time, I had discovered that the person I loved like a parent was indeed my parent. I was not adopted, as I had been brought up to believe. One might well suggest that at some deep and instinctive level, I had always known. Indeed, when the moment came and I was about to hear it from Harriet, I suddenly knew Hip was my father. I felt that it could be no other. But in the years of my childhood, it was far too shocking even to think such a thought. The nuns brainwashed us effectively to hold the clergy in uncritical awe. My mother's adamant refusal to reveal my father's identity, even as she lay dying, still daunts and puzzles me as it did Harriet and all those who knew her. Her death freed her of the burden of her secret, leaving me to carry it on.

What a perfect joke! I broke out in the kind of laughter that arises from hysterical relief. My father (just to say those words was so new and strange!) had so loved teasing Florence, and she invariably took the bait. Now that ultimate showman and center-stage character had stolen the show, her show, on the very day of her funeral. I could imagine him shaking with laughter as he welcomed her that day to the next world. Sitting by myself in the living room and taking in the import of Harriet's *Yes*, I realized that I had played a key part in a very remarkable love story.

+ + +

The drama of the day—a day in which I had buried my mother, learned at long last the identity of my father, and was finally released to openly speak the ironclad secrets of my family—was not yet played out, however. Jack, now refreshed from his nap, came down to join me for supper.

126

Jack and Florence's marriage seven years after the deaths of both his wife and Father Hip had rescued them from intense loneliness. Jack fell in love with an unusual woman with interests far wider than his life had permitted, and he was grateful to her for taking on his troubled young family and remaking a home for them. I didn't see him very often and never thought of him as my stepfather. He was always *my mother's husband*. But over the year of sharing my mother's care we had established a closer relationship during which he had, to his children's amazement, uncharacteristically opened up to me in the evenings after my mother had fallen asleep.

And so, had this mild man slapped me that evening, I could not have been more stunned by what he said as soon as we sat down to dinner. "Who the hell are you, anyway?" he demanded. "Where did you come from?" And he unleashed a tirade of long pent-up confusion and anger. With growing disbelief, I realized that he had no idea of my true relationship to my mother. They had been married for over twenty years, and she had evidently never revealed to him the fact that I was her own, not an adopted, daughter. It seemed that he and I were the only ones who hadn't known my real identity.

When I told him that she was indeed my mother, he grew even more enraged. He continued heaping his fury upon me, saying, "Well, if that's true, you were a terrible daughter!"

At the injustice of that, I called for a truce and pleaded truthfully that I was too exhausted to deal with this, that I'd had more than enough for one day, and I fled to the guest room where I went to bed too shocked even for tears.

I woke the next morning to a world that seemed eerie and unfamiliar, like a bad dream I once had in which I turned a corner on a familiar street in my town and found myself lost in a strange city. How would I face this man and deal with any further emotional shocks? When I went downstairs I was relieved to find he had already left the house to do errands.

With no one at hand to talk with and help me sort out the turmoil of the last days, I decided to call Katherine Hazen, an old friend from our years in Turkey, who lived in nearby Belmont. Hearing the desperation in my voice, she urged me to come right away to her home. In sharing with her the emotional uproar of my past forty-eight hours, I was able to regain some of my equilibrium. Katherine quickly grasped that Jack's rage had boiled over when he realized that the woman he had lived with for so long had not trusted him enough to confide in him this central fact of her life. As secrecy was my second nature, it would never have occurred to me that this was cause for his wrath.

I returned to Jack's house later in the afternoon. When he came home, he apologized contritely, truly upset by his angry outburst of the previous evening. That evening, when he said goodnight, he hugged me and called me "daughter." It is my deeply moving memory of him. He said the one thing my own father, Father Hip, could never say—and which I had longed to hear all my life.

Jack learned about my father's identity from a family member some months later. Only then did he begin to comprehend what my mother's life had been like, and to understand why she had been unable to bring herself to tell him her secrets. I was grateful for that shift. He had loved her and had taken care of her in her illness, and had put up with the bitterness that had arisen in her final years. He consulted me within the year while he was making arrangements to marry Harriet. I encouraged him and was delighted that these two people who had been so close to my mother would find comfort together.

Unfortunately, Jack's feelings toward me must have darkened again in the years that followed. When my daughter and I went to visit him on his deathbed, he was kind to her but turned his head away when I approached. I was simply a visitor at his funeral and not listed as a family member in his obituary. This was part of a pattern that had begun at my father's funeral, when I was muffled, removed from the service, and not allowed to properly grieve. Later, when my cousin Adeline died, her sister forgot to notify me, and recently when my uncle died, it did not occur to the family to contact me. I had always wished to go to his funeral and experience my father's family.

✦ ✦ ✦

In the days following the funeral, I worked on the poignant job of disposing my mother's books and personal items. Her crowded closet would, under ordinary circumstances, deter a person from penetrating its dense jumble. Her shoes, still carrying the imprint of her feet, proved especially intimate and affecting reminders. There were boxes of new and as yet unworn clothes to be given away. There were memory-laden clothes that she had not worn for years but could not part with. The intimacy of these relics of her pride in her appearance—the lingering jasmine fragrance of her Joy perfume, the imprinted shoe leather—challenged and broke down my emotional resistance for what was still to come.

At the very back of her closet, I found a green metal strong-box roughly the size of the banana and lemon breads my mother loved to bake and serve to friends. It was locked. I felt conflicted about what to do. Clearly the box was something she had hidden, yet I wanted to be open with Jack as I cleared and sorted his wife's belongings. Florence had left me her jewelry, but in going through it with her, we came across several valuable diamond rings left to her by Jack's sister; I returned them to Jack for his daughters. With that in mind, I showed him the green box, which he did

My father's metal strongbox

not recognize. I asked him if there was a cache of orphan keys kept for such a situation. He helped me look, without success, and then suggested I take it to a local locksmith. Unable to open the box while I waited, the locksmith told me to leave it with him and that he would drill it open. Several days later, I went alone to reclaim the box. I paid him and carried it back to the car to discover what it held. It was a sunny New England October afternoon as I sat there in the warm car with the box in my lap, wondering what I might find inside.

Many of us have a secret repository for the relics and the reminders of our life's hot spots, a container to open in private and to touch, to reread, to savor again the tangible souvenirs of significant connections in our life. It might be a packet of letters, old photographs, a collection of mementos, a dried flower, a ring, a legal document, a calling card. This is what I now held, drilled open after many years, newly revealed for my inspection.

The first thing I realized as I began taking out the items inside was that this was not my mother's secret repository. It was my

My father's photo of my mother and me

father's. In this box, which had probably been locked since his death in 1955, were the few intimate mementos of his secret family.

The first item in the box was a small, tan pigskin folder holding two professionally taken photographs: one of my young mother seated with her arms around a five- or six-year-old me, the other a portrait of me from the same session, outfitted in a

Father Hip (left) and friends

finely smocked polka-dotted dress with a small white linen collar, my hair curled for the occasion. The small folder was from London Harness, the Boston shop for fine leather goods. It was clear my mother had had these pictures taken as a special gift for him.

Tucked behind the pictures were three small snapshots of her that must have been favorites of his. With these pictures was a shot of him as I had never seen him, slim, standing with friends against a black car, vintage mid-1930s. He wears a clerical collar and a hat pushed back at a cavalier angle. It must have been taken when he returned from the seminary and met my mother. On a scrap of white paper, I found his pencil sketch of her in profile and several drawings of me with pigtails.

My father's drawing of me

Among the few papers, I discovered one that affirmed my status: an official document from the state of Massachusetts granting him legal guardianship of me. It was dated within months of my grand-mother Alice's death in 1942. He and Florence must have realized that should anything happen to her, this legal guardianship would give him legitimate claim to my welfare and well-being. Here was proof of the validity of my calling him *my guardian*, as I always had, without realizing that he was indeed my legal guardian, not to mention my father. With the discovery of this box, almost all the pieces of my story had finally fallen into place.

I wish I had been able to talk about its contents with my moth-er. It surely would have been a catalyst for stories, further revela-tions, and healing in both of us. But she would have been too wary to begin to discuss all that this box would bring up in her, too fear-ful of the feelings so deeply buried within her and hidden from me.

+ + +

I try to imagine my way back to early 1936 and to my mother's mindset when she discovered that she was pregnant. She was twenty-four; my father, the recently appointed young pastor of the local Polish Catholic church, was twenty-eight. My impend-ing arrival into their world must have been terrifying to her. How she told my father and Alice, my grandmother, and what the im-pact was on them, I can hardly imagine. These three very strong characters had to examine their options: to keep me or to place me for adoption. As Catholics, abortion was out of the question, and among those three players, the idea of my being given to someone else, I feel certain, would have been unthinkable. To give me up for adoption would have been, for all of them, a far easier solution, one I am glad they rejected.

My mother, ambitious to educate herself, must have seen the path ahead of her close down. She'd spent little time as a child with her strong-willed mother, who was compelled to support them as a single working woman. Florence was sent to boarding schools until she was seventeen, and farmed out to her aunts' families during holidays. She rarely mentioned her childhood to me, but an aura of loneliness and sadness permeated what she said on the few occasions it came up. She was quiet and self-contained, yet photographs of her in her late teens and early twenties show her fun-loving streak. She wore beautiful clothes, was a fast driver, and, inspired by the glamour of fledgling air travel and by Amelia Earhart and Charles Lindberg, she wanted to learn to fly. This pregnancy would change all of her dreams for herself and redirect them toward me.

In the 1930s, a premium was placed on a girl's virginity, and major scandal and shame was the lot of a woman pregnant "out of wedlock." "Fallen" women, referred to by another pejorative phrase, "damaged goods," were sent away to relatives or banished to places like the Irish Magdalen houses, where the pregnancy and birth were taken care of and the babies either given up for adoption or placed in foster care. Often, these women were rejected altogether by their families. Elaborate schemes were devised to hide this major disgrace. I remember well the Home for Little Wanderers, an orphanage in Jamaica Plain that we passed as we drove into Boston, where the children born in secrecy were sent to be cared for and hopefully adopted. Though I knew nothing about my own situation other than that I was adopted, I always looked at that building with an odd sense of connection with the little wanderers.

Secrecy was imperative. My mother's reputation was at stake, while the added and far more shocking fact of my father's priesthood sharply raised the level of disgrace for both of them. Not only a fallen woman and damaged goods, she would have been blamed and reviled for seducing a priest. My grandmother must have been immediately in on the plan they devised, or perhaps was even its mastermind, because her cooperation and support were crucial for it to work. According to the plan, my mother would spend the later months of pregnancy with her paternal grandmother and family near Trenton, New Jersey. Alice, despite her separation from Robert Fojuth, retained a close relationship with his mother. After its birth, the child would be put into foster care for its first year and then Alice would go to Philadelphia to adopt it as her own. From the little I know, this is what happened.

In this twenty-first century's open, "anything goes" society, I want to re-emphasize the intense level of shame, the ruin and disgrace that were heaped on a fallen woman and her bastard child should the truth come to light in that judgmental, straight-laced era of my childhood eighty years ago. Yet my instinct tells me that Alice supported Florence; perhaps she realized that a child would bind them more closely to each other. Perhaps it helped to alleviate Alice's fear that her daughter would marry and leave her alone. Alice adored children. It was something people consistently told me about her in later years when I asked. She had been so busy trying to stay afloat when her own daughter was small, and now my birth was a second chance for her as an attentive "adoptive" mother. I felt it. She was a warm, loving mother figure in my pre-school years, spoiling me just as an indulgent grandmother (which she indeed was) would be inclined to do.

From the beginning, my life story was woven from lies. Necessary lies of survival, lies of protection, lies covering a story that, if truthfully told, would be scandalous. This secret hung over my parents to the end of their lives. My father was a young pastor in a position that must have been an important first phase of his own ambitious trajectory. He was the oldest son in a large Polish family, the pride of his mother, and well known in the close Boston Polish community. In 1936, there could have been no serious question of his leaving the church to marry my mother. Is it possible that Florence might have asked him to leave the priesthood to marry her? I cannot imagine it one way or the other. He was already 29 at my birth, and educated for his calling. To leave the priesthood and go back to school or go into business at the depth of the Depression probably seemed unimaginable. To start a new life, they would have been compelled to leave the Boston area and go elsewhere, someplace they were not known, leaving behind their families, the greater Polish community—everything they had ever known.

+ + +

And so, Florence, pregnant with me, traveled to New Jersey, where her grandmother, Kate Foyuth, and all of her Foyuth cousins welcomed her. She developed an affectionate connection to them during her three months in Trenton. A cousin asked Florence to be godmother to a son who was born around that time. Letters were later exchanged, but I was never to meet that side of the family, though ironically, I spent my first two years of marriage in Lawrenceville, not ten miles from where members of the Foyuth family still lived. I would have welcomed knowing them, but I knew nothing of their existence then. My mother said nothing about them. When the time came, my mother went to Philadelphia to give birth, but I have no idea where or under what circumstances. After my birth in October, she placed me with a foster family somewhere in the city and returned to Norwood.

I have been unable to find any solid information about the first eight to nine months of my life; that will most likely remain a troubling void in my story. I have nothing other than the first picture of me in my mother's photograph album with "July 18, 1937," written under it. I was eight-and-a-half months old. That date, one of the few specific dates in the album, is written in my father's hand. I assume it marks the day I was brought home to Norwood to begin my life as their adopted child. In the photo I am held by Alice who is, in their cover story, my legal parent, my adoptive mother. For the first six years of my life, therefore, Florence played the role of my big sister.

I have read that the actor Jack Nicholson, born five months after me, was raised thinking his grandmother was his mother and his birth mother was his sister. They, too, were hairdressers. He

Florence, Alice and me in June of 1937—
the day I was brought home.

reportedly suffered intermittently from depression, as I did, while he worked his way through the emotional fallout of such a covert arrangement. His situation and mine were fortunate, however, as we were kept and loved. A close friend of mine, also born at the same time, had a very different experience. His pregnant mother was banished by her parents to a home for wayward women, from where, after she gave birth, her son was sent into a series of Dickensian foster homes and suffered physical and emotional abuse. He was taunted repeatedly with: "No one wants you!" John's talent was eventually recognized and he ultimately made a stellar academic career for himself. Recently, nearing 80, he wept as he told me about having found his birth family and that he had just learned that his paternal grandfather had longed for a grandson and died never knowing of John's existence. This shred of information, that someone, his own grandfather, had yearned for him and would have loved him, was enough to open a wound so old and yet still profoundly painful.

Did Florence recuperate for a while after my birth? Did she have time with her newborn daughter? Or did she return home immediately after placing me with the foster family? What story did they tell friends and family in Boston about her absence? Did they say to family and friends that she had gone to care for a sick relative or that she had had a nervous breakdown? Did Alice or

Florence travel to Philadelphia in those first months to see me? And who was the family I stayed with during that time? When I tried to find records of foster placements in Philadelphia in 1936 and '37, I was told that they hadn't been archived. It was not until I was in my fifties that I obtained an official birth certificate from the state of Pennsylvania, a document that includes no mention of either a hospital name or the names of the parents. It simply declares the birth of a girl child named Mary Alexander (sic) Fayette (sic) in Philadelphia, Pennsylvania, on October 31, 1936.

I was named Mary Alexandra Foyette after Father Hip's mother, Mary Veronica Ziolkowski, and for my grandmother, Alexandra Foyette—who became "Alice" when she separated from Robert Foyuth. I found among my mother's papers a letter to Alice from the Foyuth family, thanking her for giving over her husband's military pension to his mother, Kate. Is it possible that Alice's gift was made to them in return for having harbored my mother during her pregnancy?

+ + +

I was told that when I first began talking as a child, I referred to myself as "me, me." It stuck; my family began calling me Mimi as well as its Polish diminutive, Mimutek. Mimi remains my preferred name. I associate my given name, Mary, with my mother's infrequent bouts of anger. When she addressed me sternly as Mary! rather than Mimi or Skeezix or Pumpkin, I knew I was in trouble.

In the course of writing this memoir, I remembered another name, the odd name I had given to my imaginary childhood companion. Like many young children observing their world and trying to make sense of it through play acting and practicing how they might function out there, I had an imaginary friend. She gave me ample opportunity to try out my thoughts on a nonjudgmental sounding board of my own creation. I now realize that she was an extension of myself. The vague impression I retain sug-

Art Therapy Drawing No. 3.

gests an agreeable experience. She was always available, not to be lost or misplaced like a beloved doll. I talked with uninhibited fluidity and at length with her; imaginary or not, she was an important presence for me. I could hold forth with all my little-girl self-importance and assurance while I acted out whatever scenarios or puzzling issues or ambitions were uppermost for me to explore and experience.

What made me sit up in wonder so many years later was the ironic name I had given her: Realgirl. What soul breakthrough into a seven-year-old's imagination led me to this name? How had this strange eruption from deep within me inspired this ungainly, ungirly name? Why not Susie or Sally? If this presence, with whom I conversed animatedly in bed or in my solitary play, was the "real girl," who then, was I? Was it a child's simple wish to convince herself of this figure's validity? Or did the name point to a dawning awareness of my own complex existence? I can't begin to reconstruct the conversations we had, but their lingering aura triggers memory that floods me with rich but ephemeral sensation.

I have watched each of my granddaughters trying on different roles, and have marveled at the complete absorption and serious commitment with which they engaged in play-acting. It was my privilege, as a participant in those games, to be *their* Realgirl. With one granddaughter, I was always the Beast to her Beauty; with another I was "Sister" to be ordered about; with a third I played harried doctor to her bossy office manager. We returned again and again to these scenarios until my granddaughters outgrew them, after which these imaginary personas became a comic part of family lore.

If my companion was "Realgirl," then who was I? At that young age, I knew nothing that was real about my own story. I lived in, and embodied, the deep secret around which our family was constructed. I *was* the secret. My family was not like that of any of the families my school friends came from. I was not troubled nor do I remember feeling distress in those early years at any sense of difference. My family, such as it was, was my "normal," a loving if unconventional normal. So what seepage from my unconscious, from the inner, knowing child, suggested this name for a dear companion? It's one of the many mysteries that, despite all my delving and writing, I will have to leave unsolved.

Though we no longer converse, my imaginary friend has become an important reminder of my quest to find, late in life, a melding of Mimi and Realgirl. Have I meshed with Realgirl now that most of the mysteries are solved and the secrets revealed? My serenity leads me to think so.

✦ ✦ ✦

Sometime in my fifties, in an effort to discover something, anything, about my first nine months, I resorted to consulting a psychic. I was not averse to doing this when a friend recommended a specific person. My mother once told me of going, as a lark, to a gypsy fortuneteller when she was very young. The gypsy laid out her life in detail, saying she would meet a man who wore a kind of uniform, she would have a child, and would not marry until later in life. I have kept my grandmother's dog-eared Polish dream interpretation book. She believed in hunches, in dreams, and in laying out cards or reading tea leaves to tell fortunes. Having no details to offer the psychic, I simply asked about my first nine months in foster care.

Her emotional reaction after the reading stunned me. She described how deeply attached to me my foster mother became. She said it had been very hard for her to give me up when my family came to adopt me and take me away to Massachusetts. She said that there was another child with me in that foster home, a boy who was disabled in some way, and that I frequently heard the adults in the foster family discussing how unfortunate I had been to be left by my family. She also added that my foster mother had long since died, but that she was a steadfast spirit who continued to watch over me. This part of the reading seemed to connect with a part of the story that I was told about my adoption: the presence of the little boy. My mother and grandmother had told me they'd wanted to adopt a boy, but I was so lively and bright that they chose me instead.

I also asked her if my foster family was African-American. She couldn't say; she told me she was not able to "see" that. The question of race stems from my recollection of my mother's staunch objection to bigoted racial slurs heard in our extended family. She said to me, "Mimi, don't you ever listen to any of what you hear. I have had great kindness from Negroes." My own deeply felt response to, and instinctive familiarity and sense of comfort from, African Americans could possibly stem from those earliest months. It is merely intuitive conjecture. Another story floating in the family ether is that some arrangement was made with an African-American lawyer in Boston whose sister was a nurse in Philadelphia and had a private clinic. Did my father, who was a natural at arranging solutions to issues and difficulties, have a hand in this? Such secretive arrangements were not uncommon then. Would there have been an African-American lawyer in Boston in 1936? These queries emerge in the very fragile filaments of my memories from decades ago. I have no way of verifying what was or was not true.

Finishing my reading, the psychic broke into sobs, from which it took her some moments to recover. She kept repeating: "She really loved you, your foster mother really loved you. The bond was so strong." I had sought information and instead derived unexpected comfort from the emotional impact of the reading. It was reassuring to think I might have been well cared for and loved in that period about which I know so little.

And yet, of course, in the end, I had to leave my foster mother. Surely that separation also left its mark. We know now that infants are not the blank slates they were believed to be at the time when I was born.

> *The baby does not understand the reasons for her relinquishment, but the feelings are those of a newborn baby who simply feels the loss of a mother who never came back. The baby doesn't care why she did it: the baby just feels abandoned. And that abandoned baby lives inside each and every adoptee all his or her life.*
>
> —NANCY VERRIER, *Primal Wound*

✦ ✦ ✦

After my mother's death, and with the knowledge, at last, of my father's identity, I gradually began to think of my parents as a couple. I had never considered their life together outside of my presence. It never entered my mind that they even had such a life. Indeed, it was unthinkable with my Catholic training. Children in ordinary families witness on a day-to-day basis their parents' relationship: its affections, its disagreements, the nature of its communication. Although Father Hip came for dinner at least once a week, most of my time with my parents was spent in the midst of friends, for instance at the rectory on Sunday mornings, or alone with one or the other.

There was one exception when we traveled together as a family for two weeks. During spring vacation in 1949 when I was 13, my parents took me to Florida. We drove, stopping in Atlantic City, Williamsburg, Myrtle Beach, and Miami Beach. I did not think it odd to be on this trip with Father Hip. By now, he and I had gone together to Quebec and to New York City, but on this Florida trip, I was with both my mother and Father Hip. He was a regular part of our lives, so it did not seem strange for us to all take a vacation. At one hotel, I heard him check in under the name "Mr. Walsh"—though I didn't think anything of it. I was not asked to refrain from mentioning him when I was back in school. I simply knew that I did not talk about him in any detail in my usual chat with my friends. I was told recently by my one remaining close high school friend, Kathy, that she and another friend, Paula, had been told by Paula's father that Father Hip was my father. Like everyone else at the time, these two young teenagers never mentioned it to me or told our friends.

A favorite item in our house was a big wooden salad bowl full of matchbooks and mini match boxes that I loved to play with, arranging them by shape or color or sorting them in categories. In those days, when most people smoked, restaurants, clubs, and hotels had their presence advertised on such matchbooks, which patrons collected as a souvenir after a dinner out. I used to spend hours looking at all these matches from the Stork Club, El Morocco, various inns and restaurants, some of which I had been to with my parents. My mother did not smoke, yet she never forgot to take these keepsakes. If I did not recognize a place, she would describe it with enthusiasm. I never thought of Father Hip being there with her. It was the same with her collection of cast albums from the Broadway musicals they had seen together, *Annie Get Your Gun, Call Me Madam, Show Boat, Gentlemen Prefer Blondes,* which I listened to over and again as I grew up, later going myself to the pre-Broadway tryouts in Boston. These items—the matchbooks, the cast albums—were the evidence of their private time, their secret life together, of which I was unaware.

After her death, I found among my mother's papers some notes made on Waldorf Astoria stationery—clearly, the record of a visit she had made with Father Hip to New York City in the '40s. I glanced at them casually and then put them away. Recently, while transcribing these pages, I realized their importance and why she had kept them; they are the only record I have found of their travels. With so little time together, my parents must have looked forward to such holidays; they were both in their mid-thirties and I presume still very much in love. I was born in 1936 and I expect they'd fallen in love only the year before.

Maybe this particular trip was to celebrate the tenth anniversary of their relationship. For whatever reason, they pulled out all the stops and went for the best of everything in those two weeks. Every day they had lunch and dinner at fine restaurants, went shopping, attended the theater every evening followed by a visit to a night club or jazz club. They visited museums and they toured the city. For example, on the 14th of August, 1945, they had breakfast in bed, went to the Metropolitan Museum, had dinner at Chambord, and saw a performance of *Carousel*. My mother's final note for that day says simply, "Walked through Times Sq. (Peace)." It was V-J Day, the end of World War II. They had been there in the crowds with those iconic sailors jubilantly kissing the women they encountered. Away at summer camp, I was aware of the import of this day, because many campers and counselors wept, knowing that their fathers and brothers would be returning, or not. But I had no idea my parents were walking amid the elated crowds in Times Square.

Their secret relationship must have brought an exciting edge to their lives, at least at times. They didn't have to put up with the daily irritants of a formal marriage, and I have no memory or impression of anger between them. Both were bright and curious with a very good sense of humor. He was from a large, lively family, while she was more restrained and used to the solitude of an only child. They were both book lovers and both loved to prowl for antiques. He was especially fond of late nineteenth-century watercolors and oils. Each of them served the community and was important and respected there. I would say, in retrospect, that they were well matched. Florence occasionally went out with other men, and perhaps that served the charade of her status as a single woman. Some of the men persisted in their pursuit, perhaps unable to understand why such a woman was not married. What my father thought about her admirers, I have no idea. They conducted separate, busy lives and had their own friends, homes, and demanding work. Their love lasted until his death in 1955.

I have been asked many times, *Why didn't they marry and make a normal life for you? Aren't you enraged that you were forced to live in secret like that?* Well, I have no idea of what they decided or discussed around that issue. Maybe he offered and she refused, as she had a thriving business that supported us well. Maybe she asked and he couldn't see a way of supporting a family, the Great Depression barely over. Perhaps he couldn't face deflating his mother's pride in him and his sacred vocation. All I know in the end is that, having sinned in the eyes of the Catholic Church, they courageously faced the consequences of their action and, being in love, took the risk of keeping me and raising me together.

Father Hip was very much in the picture as father figure, disciplinarian, and co-provider of the myriad benefits of my childhood: summer camp; art classes at the Museum of Fine Arts; visits to the symphony and theater, to New York City and Quebec, to Braves and Red Sox games. I spent many afternoons with him prowling the antique shops in Boston, and was thus prepared for the riches of the Istanbul Bazaar. I was also exposed to a large cross-section of people in my mother's shop and through my guardian's wide array of friends. My family, so unlike others in town, was unusual in that my parents took pains to expose me to the world beyond Norwood. My upbringing was, I am convinced, more eclectic than those of my friends and schoolmates. As I realized much later, this unlikely couple had prepared me well for the life I began to lead in college and later in my globe-trotting marriage.

PART FOUR

*For the unlearned, old age is winter; for the learned,
it is the season of the harvest.*

—HASIDIC SAYING

What I knew until 1971

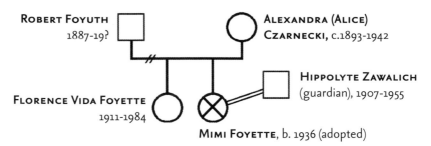

ROBERT FOYUTH
1887-19?

ALEXANDRA (ALICE)
CZARNECKI, c.1893-1942

HIPPOLYTE ZAWALICH
(guardian), 1907-1955

FLORENCE VIDA FOYETTE
1911-1984

MIMI FOYETTE, b. 1936 (adopted)

What I knew from 1971–1984

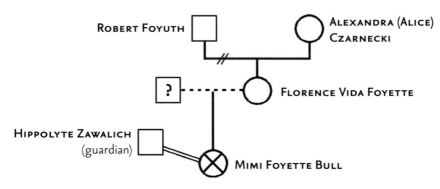

ROBERT FOYUTH

ALEXANDRA (ALICE)
CZARNECKI

?

FLORENCE VIDA FOYETTE

HIPPOLYTE ZAWALICH
(guardian)

MIMI FOYETTE BULL

What I have known since 1984

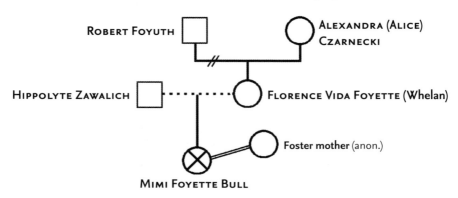

ROBERT FOYUTH

ALEXANDRA (ALICE)
CZARNECKI

HIPPOLYTE ZAWALICH

FLORENCE VIDA FOYETTE (Whelan)

Foster mother (anon.)

MIMI FOYETTE BULL

THE 1980S MARKED A NEW ERA in my husband's professional life. We had bought a house in Princeton, and after thirty years as a teacher and headmaster in independent schools, he decided to establish his own consulting business. Now in his mid-fifties, Neil cut loose from working with academic institutions and went out on his own. He had realized that his two years in the Navy before enrolling at Princeton University in 1946 were critical to his education. That unusual break, after what he termed the "normal lock-step progress of American education," gave him a more mature and prepared mind for higher education. He had also met a lot of Peace Corps volunteers in Turkey who had commented on the life-altering nature of their work, and he had seen, first-hand, the impact made on Verde Valley School students by their annual trips to Mexico and to Native American reservations.

His new business, the Center for Interim Programs or, simply, Interim, was born from the shoebox into which he had been tossing ideas and names of people working on diverse projects in interesting locations. He began informally putting together gap years for our children, for children of friends in Princeton, and the idea spread rapidly by word of mouth. A fellow Princeton alumnus of Neil's, a member of the *New York Times* Ochs Sulzberger family, saw a three-line notice in the *Princeton Alumni Weekly* describing what Neil was doing and, his interest piqued, asked his education editor to investigate. Neil was swamped with phone calls when the resulting article appeared in January of 1981.

That single article would generate work for years to come. Neil did go out to ring the church bell by speaking at schools all around the country, and we traveled a good deal looking at potential programs for his clients. He was an irresistible and irrepressible spokesman for an idea that people were initially slow to embrace. Charisma is an overworked word, but Neil epitomized it in his natural showmanship and charm. There was not a self-conscious bone in his body. As had always been the case, he loved working with kids and Interim gave him a whole new angle for engaging them and opening up possibilities to them. Always a fount of ideas, always unconventional, and always sound in his work, he found his métier in Interim and lived long enough to see that his intrepid promotion of the gap year concept led to it becoming an established part of American education.

✦ ✦ ✦

The late 1980s brought new beginnings for both Neil and me. The problem was that we were headed in opposite directions: his energies and attention were, as ever, directed outward, while mine were pointed inward, with a determination I had never felt before. He was absorbed with the task of founding Interim, while I, armed with the newly acquired truths of my childhood, was starting to confront and focus on the depression that had hobbled me for so long. I began to face what I had always feared and dreaded and instinctively protected myself against—namely, exposure. Lot of things were bubbling to the surface and I was struggling to maintain my equilibrium, but when I needed Neil's understanding and support he grew upset and angry because I was not there for *him*. It makes sense now that I look back on it, but at the time his reaction served only to bury my impulse to speak out. Each time this happened it got worse and I felt more and more depressed and alone. I can take someone's emotional temperature from a glance or a phrase on the telephone, and I expected him to recognize my pain even as I busily worked to hide it from him. Sheer idiocy all around. We both concealed our feelings. Or he stormed around like an angry chimpanzee making diversionary noises to hide his confusion while I retreated further and further into myself.

Journal entry, January 1988: I have been fighting ineffectively for my own autonomous physical and emotional space. It is clear that I am in limbo between the person I was and the person that has to emerge, the person Ben has been awaiting and the person the kids have pushed for. The person I long to be.

CAMBRIDGE, MASSACHUSETTS

In 1987, thinking that we would use it as a weekend and summer retreat, we bought a house in New Hampshire. But after a couple of years we tired of the long commute between Princeton and Peterborough and moved north to take up residence in a large condo near Harvard Square.

Living in Cambridge presented me with the chance to at last make a deliberate career choice rather than settle for whatever job might be available. While I'd had some unexpected and challenging work and a good measure of success, now I wanted to take an innate ability, train it for a profession, and see where it would take me. Having decided to go to graduate school, I began to look at master's degree programs in greater Boston. My inclination was to go into the fledgling field of geriatric counseling. Lesley College (now Lesley University) did not offer this specialty, but the faculty there agreed that I could tailor my courses to my chosen field in their Counseling Psychology program. I could do my required apprenticeships in hospice work and in nursing homes. Lesley's atmosphere appealed to me, and it was within walking distance of our apartment on Concord Avenue.

My resolve to heal manifested in a variety of ways. My mother's death prompted me to begin keeping a journal and, after learning my father's identity, I wrote my way through the impact of these events. Having derived great benefit from the two Progoff seminars I had taken in Princeton, I participated in two more in Cambridge. The Progoff system provided me with an organized framework within which to question and probe every part of my life. I had worked fruitlessly with a variety of therapists until I learned about Tom Cottle, a Boston psychotherapist. After reading his excellent book on family secrets and their impact on children, I contacted him and began a course of therapy that lasted several years. My kids sent me to an assortment of encounter groups, but I found that these were of minimal value to me, whose life story and experience were so different from those of my fellow participants. Yet all these efforts had something to offer in the slow process of removing my armor. As for antidepressants, I chose to avoid them, fearing that they might change my sensibility or blunt the very drive to heal that would have made me take them in the first place.

My program at Lesley College proved to be another important escape route from depression. The nature of my coursework made me face the fact that, to be a good therapist, I had to speak, I had to reveal myself. I could no longer get by simply as the observer. In all the travels of my young adulthood, in marriage, in parenting, in being a headmaster's wife, and, what's more, having no siblings to consult—in all these I'd had to quickly master the art of survival, learn how to hit the ground running and how not to fail. I learned all too well to keep my own counsel and solve my problems alone or bury them inside. Early on at Lesley, in a class on Group Dynamics, my resistance and reserve were repeatedly challenged by my much younger classmates. I had to break open in order to work with others and accept their help. I realized that, like a non-swimmer thrown into deep water, I was being forced to learn how to save myself. So I remain grateful to my young Lesley classmates for their persistence and affectionate drive in getting me to speak, in "outing" me in that safe place. That experience, initially so threatening and difficult, was instrumental in my breakthrough. To open up and join the human comedy was so much easier than I had imagined. Free of the primal fear of rejection by my unwitting parents and of being sent back to the orphanage for being less than perfect, I could finally begin to speak the unspeakable.

✦ ✦ ✦

Art Therapy Drawing No. 4—The Red House

For this drawing, each class member was told to imagine his or her life as a fairy tale. Following are the notes I jotted down to accompany the drawing.

This is a story of a child born deep in an ancient wood. It was familiar and not a frightening wood. But it was full of darkness & mystery. The paths were not marked. The child had to learn and read the signs and remember the landmarks in order to find her way out. She knew she was guided & cared for but it was an inner knowing. One day in her journey out of the wood, she came to a beautiful clearing with a pool. She dove into the clear water and scooped up handfuls of tiny carved ivory and jewels that made up the bottom of the pool. She emerged with ivory, jade, gold figures tumbling from her palms. She knew she was near the end of the wood. Beyond, a path lay to a red house which would be hers. She knew when she saw it that she would be home.

✦ ✦ ✦

Journal entry, February 3, 1988: Productive session with Cottle. He told me that after reflection, he decided that he knew who I was, the daughter of God! What an interview for Barbara Walters. He outlined all the anger a child would feel in my situation—that I had chosen to look at the nobility of the facts and to hold on to the tenuous and forged "passport" that I held. I was very likely full of rage, and helplessness over what a predicament I had been placed in—lied to about everything and thereby denied so much. While it was hard to feel what he was describing—my gut began to churn. And at home by the fire—a bit of emotion began to come, and that night I could get very little and fitful sleep.

Journal entry, December 7, 1990: I am in touch with the reality at least of Ben. It is now twenty years that I have known him, having met him in the fateful 1970-71. Embedded in that relationship is the forbidden, the secretive, the father figure, the priest. He is the one who recognized me, the authentic me. He has not gone away. He is perhaps a reflection of my first family, if, as I suspect,

I was in a black foster family in Philadelphia. . . . Although I have been acting out the dysfunctional aspects of my childhood, I would hate to think of my life without Ben. In some sense he kept Realgirl alive. . . .

So I scream and rant and yell and curse at how all the good intentions and choices of my parents have warped my life and forced me to live a sham, acted, façade so invidious and so subtle that I have not been aware of the poison except in the "nameless" depressions and the sense of not being able to express myself, not being able to unblock a lot of energy, not being able to fulfill potential that everyone else sees and I know is somewhere buried within. They made choices they could live with, but which I in my real personness could not. That person got edited out, embodied in an imaginary playmate, and faded away. For my sake, and ultimately for their own, they should have been honest about themselves and me, gotten married and at least given me tangible parents, and not a tissue, not a quagmire of lies that gave me no firm basis on which to build a self. No childhood. Forgetful, living in the present—unmindful of the chasms of danger that revelation of some unspeakable secret would drop us into. I write all this, and my heart rate is steady, my head is clear, and I feel not a thing. Numbness is another thing to thank you for. Indecision, confusion, mild agoraphobia, morning panic are the daily reminders. . . .

Next step is to get at feelings that are safely embedded in layers and layers of denial secure enough to withstand atomic leakage. I *am* afraid of letting it out. . . .

+ + +

Weekends, holidays, and vacations, we went to the farm. I'd discovered it in 1986, when I was in New Hampshire visiting a friend. Coming down a back road into Peterborough, I'd seen, and instantly fallen for, a red house that sat directly on the road. It had no view, no nearby pond or stream, but it spoke to me. It evoked all the memories of driving in the countryside with my mother, who loved early New England houses. I knew she would have loved this one. Built like a fortress in 1790 by early settlers, it was a classic New Hampshire Cape, painted barn red with white trim, its interior very much as it was when it was built, with wide pine floorboards and a large, central fireplace. The cellar foundation was constructed with boulders only oxen could have managed. It was not a rational, well-researched purchase, but the result of an instant affinity on my part.

Our professional life had provided us with a variety of houses that we adapted to: from the adobe house in the red rock country near Sedona to the large villa apartment in Vienna overlooking the Vienna Woods to the 1950s' Doris Day ranch house and pool in San Antonio— all the places we landed in and made our own. We spent ten years in our Princeton house, where Interim was started. Our Cambridge condo was, for another ten years, home and office and a possible place to retire, but rejected as such when I chose, after my husband's death, to settle in Peterborough.

The red house was my first chosen home. It gathered in our books, our carpets from Turkey, all the odds and ends from our travels and from our families, and gave us an old garden, a big barn, woods, and friendly neighbors, and it was blessed on all sides with a medley of old stone walls. Neil, an avid if untutored putterer, found endless projects to attack, enjoying the trips to the hardware store and the dump that such endeavors generated. Our granddaughters came to spend time picking blueberries, swimming, sleeping in the alcove above the stairs, and climbing on nearby Mt. Monadnock, which dominates and gives its name to this region. Our friends came to feast with us, to rest and relax and sleep well within the house's old walls.

I bought the red house as quickly and instinctively as I'd agreed to marry Neil. Within hours of first encounter. I bought it as I was unraveling my past and reweaving my story. It housed me through the worst of my suicidal spells and now shelters my full and contented old age. The house is like a wonderfully comfortable denim shirt: broken in, presentable, and the one you always reach for. Like all of one's beloveds, it gives me some unpleasant surprises, untimely demands, but it more than compensates with what my husband called "psychic income." There is most certainly a spirit of place—perhaps a rich accumulation of good vibrations left by people who owned it happily before us. I have often been in places that are, on the surface, attractive, but have no deeper sense of place. It is more than charm; it is more than conventional beauty. It is a good genie that dwells here and makes me happy. I share it with a variety of local wildlife whose forebears have been here much longer than me: woodchucks, chipmunks, field mice, an occasional skunk or porcupine, lady bugs who winter over tucked in corners, snakes who keep to themselves and discreetly hold some of the above population in check. Local turkeys and deer and now and again bear, fox, and coyote roam my property, a noisy family of crows lives nearby, and once a solitary moose was chased away by our dog.

I was surprised several years ago to find a wish list I once made about what I would want from my ideal home. The red house checks off the important characteristics I listed so long ago and is a haven that I will eventually leave after years of contented life here.

+ + +

In the outermost realm of pain and isolation brought on by self-loathing and the conviction that everyone would be better off without me, my thoughts turned from time to time to suicide. Somewhere in the confusion of this wretched pain were the words of the helpless child: *I am the cause of your trouble. I am the scarlet letter, the living evidence of your sin. I need to do away with it/myself.* These words were not consciously expressed. I simply had a sense that things would be better if I were gone. The huge barrier to achieving this was the realization that I could not leave my children or husband with this legacy, though I spent hours trying to figure a way of disappearing without violence and without a trace. Because I could not bring myself to speak to anyone about my suicidal attacks, I had no measure, no frame of reference. It was not until I read William Styron's *Darkness Visible*, a book about Styron's battle with his depression, that I realized how serious my own was.

Neil was no help, and even Ben was without understanding or support. Accustomed to commanding the pulpit, he was invariably hard to deal with on this subject. I recall a conversation of ours turning into a shouting match as I tried to get his head turned around to thinking of depression as a physiological problem, not just a mental condition of the weak who can't deal with their lives. This profound and painful and debilitating disease was so hidden and so misunderstood at the time that getting any sort of recognition or assistance was very difficult.

> **Journal entry, April 1990:** Holly has stayed with me [through this difficult stretch of suicidal depression] and made an astute but quite obvious observation that has eluded me all these years. She said: *Mom, you were trying to destroy your parents' secret, namely you.* My solution to these traps and corners when I feel impotent and useless, and worse that it would be better without me, harks back to very old stuff. Since I was the obvious result, the evidence of a difficult situation, the ever-present

reminder to my mother and father of what they did to alter their lives and trap them and brand them, my answer was to do away with the evidence, i.e. myself, and thereby that things would be better for everyone without me. I have very easily continued that solution or truth whenever things get bewildering or difficult or out of my control. I don't basically want to do this (suicide) but the urge is all but overwhelming and logical in the atmosphere of this world I find myself in, and makes it seem the only answer. I have never thought of this as a lifelong response, but of course it is something I learned and figured out as a child and it makes eminent sense. The effort to get beyond it, to avoid this inevitable course of events, has kept me exhausted and has sapped a major part of my energy and a major part of my aspiration. *What is the use of doing anything of substance? It will only lead to your getting in the way, your standing in the progress of others.* When I begin to feel worthwhile, this potent reminder of REALITY gets right in there and sabotages any sense of worth I might begin to formulate for myself. It is a repetitive and seemingly inevitable pattern. It is the source of my lack of drive. What is the use of aiming for something when you will find that *you* are the monster in the works, that you are destroying life for others? It is a clear barrier, an old stumbling block, an old habit which I have never recognized and therefore can stumble over again and again. Destroying myself is the only logical solution to the pain I feel.

Whoever I am or might have been is lost in the protected façade that I have built to enable me to function from day to day. It has turned me into a depressive personality, it has turned me into the observer, into the one who is afraid to risk and plunge in. I watch the dance, I watch the adventure, and I take vicarious pleasure in the dance, and eternally await my turn.

+ + +

I begin to examine the less obvious but relentless details of depression now that I think of getting relief. I realize that what I consider feeling normal still carries daily vestiges of depression that those who know nothing of its blight would not tolerate. I awaken at 6:00 a.m. with gripping fear in my gut, not linked to anything specific but simply there to be banished and fought through and appearing before any conscious thought has had a chance to generate it. Simply a nameless fear upon waking which casts the initial pall over the day and must be shoveled aside like a heavy, wet snow before the day's adventure can be undertaken.

—WILLIAM STYRON, *Darkness Visible*

After reading Styron's clear and brilliant description of depression, I gained a tremendous respect for my own nearly superhuman strength in overcoming thirty years of its attacks and, in the process, both carrying on some sense of normalcy and managing to climb out of ever-increasing and powerful assaults. I shared with Styron the nameless morning fear, and developed the habit of propelling myself out in the morning for breakfast, a habit I continue. At some point, I realized it was less costly than a therapist. Because they started with the death of my father in the mid-1950s, when such things as depression and "nervous breakdown" were spoken of in hushed tones or not spoken of at all, I kept these pains to myself, drove them deeper within, and battled alone.

Journal entry, January 1992: I bought a mirror yesterday (i.e., the day before making this drawing). It reminded me of when I feared not seeing a reflection. It reminded me of my great dream of the forest pool—of diving through the reflection, or into it, and down to the jewels below. It reminded me of searching in mirrors [for] the mystery of my face—who was I? where did I come from?—and not seeing it.

Art Therapy Drawing No. 5

Journal entry, December 12, 2018: This particular drawing continues to upset me viscerally. I look at it with sadness and compassion for that younger depressed self. It is a vivid sketch of me during a bout of depression—sick under the surface and putting on a "happy face" while struggling to meet the demands of a busy life.

The essential kernel of my depression was a secret I did not know. But, like a seeded oyster, it slowly built a black pearl, toxic, degenerative, chronic, releasing the pain in incremental doses of bewildering debility. Through history, illnesses such as leprosy, the plague, AIDS, and madness condemned individuals to isolation as they were shunned and cast out by their communities. With my hidden depression, I cast myself out. I was ashamed, bewildered, and isolated. I could not admit, describe, or share what ailed me; it would be years into my adult life before I learned its secret root cause. By then, in the late 1980s, social attitudes toward mental illness had begun to change, and after many false starts, I found compassionate counsel with Tom Cottle. I also broke out of my shell of isolated secrecy and, with relief, began to assemble and tell myself and others my true story. Of all the various trials of life, I am most grateful to be relieved of the intermittent and ever more intense depth of this suicidal mindset.

✦ ✦ ✦

Within months of my mother's death and discovering the identity of my father, and having, in essence, the full story, I felt free to broadcast the whole truth. I had a startling story to tell and a physical urge to share it, and I relished the disbelief among my friends and the rapt engagement of new acquaintances as I told it. The truth of my situation was no longer a disgrace. I could speak it openly now and, what's more, I no longer had to spare the feelings of a questioner. One friend was so moved that he burst into tears. All too aware of the lack of mystery in his own life and feeling, he said, like he knew it all, he was momentarily lost in the wonder of someone being given, in middle age, a whole new life story. He said, "Mimi, you have the rare chance to redo your identity at this stage of your life." It was an unexpected and lovely new perspective on my situation.

One of the most important people I talked to was my uncle

Edmund, Father Hip's kid brother, whom I had known as a child. We had not been in touch since Pate's death. When I called he immediately invited me to visit him.

> **Journal entry, April 24, 1985:** Glorious reunion with Edmund. He was waiting for me on the front walk, looking like a bull —with a wonderful Hemingway beard and a broad barrel chest. I suddenly realized where Sam got his. We went inside after a big warm hug and I sat facing him—and wept. He said he was glad we had met again after all these years. I asked him if he knew why I'd come. He wasn't sure. I told him I had discovered who my father was when Mother died. And he said that of course he'd always suspected it, that when he first saw me I had Zawalich all over my features. He said that while waiting for me to arrive, the thought had occurred to him that he might be welcoming a family member.

Edmund's warm response was critical. Other priests' children have been rebuffed when approaching newly discovered family members, and I would have been utterly wounded had that been the case with me. Edmund's daughter Susan and his sons and their families were generous as well, and reached out without reserve. When their cousin Janice Forbes, who lived in Idaho, heard about me, she wrote a loving letter offering her warm welcome as well. She remembered when Father Hip, her godfather, and I had made a visit to her family's dairy farm when the two of us were children.

A few years later, in the 1990s, I went through a phase when sudden visceral anger would course through me if I saw a priest in a public place dining with a woman. I wanted to confront them— with I frankly don't know what—and vent a nameless anger that made my heart pound. Such incidents, which were few, took me by surprise. Once, on a whim, I looked up the phone number for the chancery office of the Boston Catholic Diocese. The revelations in the *Boston Globe* of how the church had protected priests who were abusing children were hitting their mark. I wanted to pile on an added bit of discomfort to the wounded behemoth, or maybe I simply wanted to make myself known as one of their bastards swept way under the carpet. A prim operator answered and asked me what my business might be so that she could transfer me to the proper party. I said I simply wished to inquire if they conducted support groups for children of priests. Dead silence on the other end. I waited, savoring my initial fix from this first reaction. While on hold, I visualized a huddle of clergy deciding whom to set in defensive play.

The answer arrived as a scholarly, soothing voice came on line to say that no, there was no such group, in a manner effectively closing the discussion. There was no inquiry as to my reason for asking and no offer of counsel or assistance. It amounted to a final, impersonal, and civil kiss-off by my Mother Church or, perhaps more aptly, Father Church.

In the unlikely chance that they did conduct such a group, I would have quickly abandoned my cheeky prank and asked to join. My impulse had not been serious. I had wanted to poke fun at the august, under-siege Boston diocese. The irreverent call satisfied me and gave me a small-minded fix. Yet there still remained an unsatisfied need to connect and be recognized by the church that was my world until I finally made a break at thirty-five.

I had never had the chance to meet others who grew up in a priest's secret family. I have been in touch with a woman whose married father was a former priest, but that is light years away in experience from my own. The enormous burden of toxic secrecy, the lack of any sense of one's true identity, the limbo of one's place in the world make it a different story.

I suspect that the diocese knew about me. The best evidence is that my father, a talented and charismatic priest, was never transferred to a larger parish or a more important post. I was told by Lil Fraser, who cared for me as a child and was a close friend of Father Hip, that at one point, he had his bags packed, ready to move to an available and prestigious assignment he fully expected. It didn't happen. That may have been his punishment. I doubt the Church had any compassionate thought of my well-being in keeping him nearby in his small Norwood parish.

He took me, when I was in high school, to meet then-Archbishop Cushing at his residence near Boston College. We knocked on the door, which was opened by the archbishop himself, genial and welcoming. Was this a spontaneous visit on my father's part? I was in awe and don't recall anything other than the fact of the visit and that the archbishop informally opened the door to us himself. He later came to speak at my graduation ceremony at Holy Cross Academy, which he had founded with the Sisters of Holy Cross.

Me, Archbishop Cushing, Mother, May 1954

My father paid a big price for me. He lived to see me well on my way: he visited me at Smith College, where I was happily established as a freshman. He was clearly proud of the love child that he and Florence had chosen to keep. He died too young, at forty-seven, of stroke and heart attack. He smoked, he drank, he loved to eat, he worked extremely hard; and yet, there must have been an inner anguish of frustrated ambition from having been bound to his small playing field. I speculate. I don't know.

It took me a couple of years to get over this novelty of telling my story, this thrill of utter release from the bondage of circumspection. I felt like a CIA operative who might find herself free at last to explain what she had been up to for years. I was again reminded, several years later, of the impact of the years of secrecy when I took my elderly cousin Lidia to Poland on two visits to our family there. Because she was unable to deal with my true identity, I remained, for her sake, Florence's adopted daughter. When meeting our Polish relatives, it was incumbent on me to maintain that degree of separation. In such situations, where one visits relatives in another country, they are interested in their own blood relatives, given the brief nature of the visits. So, once again in a role I had been released from, I was constrained to become the nice, but not really connected, bit of family history. In such a situation, the words "bar sinister"—the heraldic phrase indicating bastardy— really feels sinister. It suited Lidia to be the center of attention, and for me, knowing that at her advanced age this could well be the last such gathering, it was fine to go along with the pretense. But it meant donning once more the straightjacket of secrecy.

One significant image that arose, alongside the anger I described earlier, was that of the Japanese bonsai. Given the radical way that a bonsai is pruned and formed, it was easy to compare myself to one. A friend once made such a comparison when she said my story was one of "a passionate soul under house arrest." In a journal entry from the period, I wrote that:

Rather than sitting in a pot on somebody's shelf, I would rather be a full flowering tree in the landscape, as I was meant to be. It makes me anxious to think that it might be too late to change. But in a sense it never is; even a bonsai must have its roots continually cut to keep it dwarfed. The Chinese were the ones to bind women's feet—it is the same impulse as pruning roots. To take a powerful force and dwarf it and subjugate it—the woman, the tree. In both cases, the reduction of the object's reach or span for one's pleasure. My goal in life may be to free all the bonsai trees. Get 'em out of their bowls and plant them in an open, lush woodland. We could sell T-shirts. *Free the Bonsai!*

+ + +

I was disappointed to realize that knowing my father's identity did not solve my depression. Barnacles of other issues from my life encrusted and muddied any solid resolution for me. My marriage was complicated; my long term mentor/love relationship with Ben entered into the mix I needed to gain the recognition I craved. All of these facets of my middle-aged life denied me the simple on/off light switch solution I expected. Much hard work lay ahead. I would soon learn an important lesson before embarking on my next work.

While in Princeton in the '80s, I had spent time in Baltimore taking care of one of my husband's Lawrenceville students, a man named Larry Glass whom I had met in 1959 when he was living as a graduate student in the Albert Einstein house in Princeton. Larry was a brilliant and erratic poet and composer who, after a promising career in finance, had suffered a head injury in an automobile crash that left him psychologically impaired. He lived alone, an eccentric isolate, in a great old Baltimore mansion. He called us one day in distress as I was setting out to visit our daughter at the

University of Virginia, and I told him that I would stop in as I passed through Baltimore.

I rang the bell of his house in Mt. Vernon Place and found myself facing a middle-aged man dressed to the waist like a French aristocrat (which I think he searched his genealogy to affirm) and from there down in baggy sweatpants and combat boots. The house displayed a crumbling elegance as he led me through its six floors. It was like an institute for scholars. He had separate libraries for literature, medicine, music, genealogy, art, and architecture. Around these were apartments with unused facilities, empty rooms, and, at the top, one of the most beautiful attics I had ever seen, with a panoramic view of the city and its harbor. Afraid of the city's rising crime rate and aware that his formidable mind had been compromised, he had retreated into his castle, a place in which time had stopped in his world of 1950s New York.

During my visit, I agreed I would return to help him. Larry ignored his mail and his bills, needed to make some medical appointments, and generally would benefit from some outside care. Ultimately, I was able to accomplish some practical things and serve as a liaison with his trust officer and his mother.

Larry gave me a very direct friendship. He remained a warm-hearted, observant pal who was uncanny in picking up my mindset and listening to what I expressed. And he pressed me to write, to speak out. As isolated and self-absorbed and eccentric as he was, he was a most valued and emotionally generous friend. When he was well, he was outrageously amusing company. In taking the risk and committing time to his care, I was the fortunate benefactor. He became a close friend, the best of company in the times when he was not shut away in black despair. What I learned from my years of experience with him was that I could not save him. I could listen and be present for him. This lesson gave me a major advantage when I began to work with the elderly.

Journal entry, Baltimore, March 1987: Before I leave the shadows of [Larry's] house, I have to catch the images that haunt. Outside noises: traffic sirens, junkies, and street people. Dying energy against restored and empty buildings. Silence dust books piles of supplies notes files desks and lights set up for work that is elegant and tortured and dwindling to a stop. The balloon in the cranium dragging the carcass about. Multi-faceted multi-faced. Byzantine, sweet beyond words, haunted, fine lapsing from the naughty imp to the vacant sad man. Chambers and rooms and passages of the mind, memories, poems, projects, disappointments, tragedies, lost books, destruction, and talents turned to fiendish, distorted hatred expressed in beyond-the-spectrum refinements. Life beyond one's talents, life half lived, talent destroyed and death beyond the living work. Freud asks for Work and Love. What has happened here?

The meticulous mind unnerved by delaying doctors, slowed by the retreat of the Parnate and by his lack of hope, sees the hopelessness of keeping the house together by himself and sees the resulting deterioration, dust, disorder as the mode of his own dissolution.

+ + +

I apprenticed at Cambridge Hospital's Geriatric Services for the Lesley degree practicum. It grew into a permanent job that I loved. I was at last doing something I chose, that I was trained for, and that I found to be a thoroughly satisfying challenge. The Geriatric Services evolved at the time when many of the state residential psychiatric facilities were closed, when the development of psychotropic medication allowed most of the once-institution-alized patients to live on their own. Patients who had been confined to these institutions for years needed help in transitioning to life outside, as well as scheduled supervision to see that they were taking their medication regularly. In time, the Geriatric Services expanded to include elderly patients suffering age-related isolation, loneliness, suicidal depression, grief, and loss. Our patients were mainly homebound or in nursing homes, and I soon had a caseload that took me all over Cambridge and Somerville into a full spectrum of lives. Visiting them where they lived as opposed to a carefully staged office setting required a very different sort of therapy. I learned from them, letting *them* take the lead in how much they could reveal, and at what pace. My case notes, which were later added to the nursing home files, helped the overworked staff to better understand who their patients were as individuals, and as a result they were (ideally) treated with more respect and insight. My clients, a generation older than me, were as familiar to me as the people I grew up with in my home town. They taught me the value of addressing some of the important, often avoided, tasks of the final stage of life: life review, appreciation for what one has accomplished, and forgiveness for the human failings—one's own and others'. Such work could go a long way to easing their fears about dying.

+ + +

It was inevitable that the person I became under the habit and strictures of ironbound secrecy would impact my parenting in more ways than I can determine and, in particular, in my response to the differences among my three children. During the first years of my marriage, when they were born, I experienced dramatic changes. Straight out of college, I moved into the very different world of the boy's prep school, living in a dormitory with a husband who largely reverted, in the first two years, to his bachelor life and was steeped in his duties as housemaster, history teacher, wrestling coach, and skeet coach. Within two years, with a second son on the way, I prepared to move to Turkey, where I would learn to run a house under quite different conditions, assume the role of headmaster's wife, and produce a third child at twenty-six. The children arrived to a young mother with her hands full, who was beginning to suffer intermittent attacks of depression that left her bewildered and which she desperately tried to hide.

This is from a letter I wrote to my son Neil in November 1986:

> I think that as much as the negativity that has circulated in me about myself, the necessity of keeping the secret, of being its subject, object and ultimately its victim—all this has blocked my own willingness to engage and to let out what creativity I had. I keep coming up with the image of the bonsai; one can create such an exquisite botanical oddity but it has none of the glory of a great, unfettered tree. I feel that my roots were trimmed, literally, and that I held back as a result. The holding back, the "self-censorship," as May Sarton puts it, is the worst thing for an artist. "To deny what one is," she observes, "is ultimately to postpone life and creativity." Embodying this observation of Sarton's, I emerged as a person who will regret only what I did not do, along with the mistakes I did not feel free to make. It was what it was.

While a student at Princeton, son Sam began acting out, and at one point presented me with a computer printout listing my shortcomings as a mother. The shock of receiving that list, as well as other brewing family issues I cannot now recall, prompted me to find a good family therapist. During our first meeting, he pointed out that when one member of the family is in the spotlight, he/

With my children on the steps of the Scott House, our residence during the six years in Turkey. In the Fall of 1996 we all gathered in Istanbul to celebrate my sixtieth birthday and took the opportunity to revisit the campus of the former Robert Academy, now Bosphorus University, as well as the house we had left thirty years before (now an administrative office building).

she is often protecting someone else. "Who is Sam protecting?" he asked. Without exception, they all turned to me. Our few meetings with the therapist over the next months opened up rich conversation in the family, relieved Sam of his pressure, and forced me out into the open, to begin to speak.

I was hardly aware of the impact made on the other members of the family by my reticence, my inscrutability, my circumspection. Such inhibition had formed a despotic self-government I could not easily overthrow. At one point, my son Neil wrote to me:

> The irony is—for someone who can express themselves so eloquently in writing—to be such a brooder on secrets. Do I speak of you or of me? Sam and I were talking about you last night, the influence you have had on us, how your silence and depression shaped us, how we still carry you.

✦ ✦ ✦

Visiting hospitals and nursing homes as a geriatric counselor made me subject to serial respiratory infections, always my Achilles heel. To bolster my immune system, my daughter Holly suggested I see her Brookline acupuncturist, Joe Burstein. Several months into his treatment, Joe mentioned that in reviewing my medical history he noticed my years of intermittent depression. He said that, if I were willing, he had an acupuncture protocol for depression to which certain people—not everyone, he emphasized—responded very well. Within a month, I began to feel the difference; it was clear and dramatic. The gray film of emotional numbness lifted and was replaced by feelings of joy, anger, humor, and sadness of an intensity I hadn't experienced for years. Since I have always refused to take any antidepressants, I feel confident in saying that acupuncture was the final straw that broke the back of the depression. Therapy, my extensive probing journals, my children's urging, the deep work at Lesley—all had made me a prime and positive subject for this course of treatment. I can say, in all honesty and without exaggeration, that since that treatment late in 1996, when I was turning sixty, I have never again experienced a moment of depression.

+ + +

Neil was always more involved in his work and public life than his private world. If there was a choice, he always opted for the next encounter, the new person over the intimate exchange. In this we were opposites. He invariably put aside the private conversation for the encounter with a stranger. I never could accept this and I simply swallowed the hurt. I wanted his undivided attention when I had him to myself. If I *did* object, he did not understand my anger, my irrational feeling that I was not interesting enough to hold his attention. He was always ready to be "on" for a new audience. That was hard to accept; it felt obliterating. There was no graceful way to object without sounding like a wimpy whiner. It took me nearly our entire life together to hit him with a metaphorical two-by-four and demand his focus. He loved it when I finally did so, although he had to absorb decades of pent-up anger—which he did with surprising grace. I expect he was as frustrated with my ability to absorb his short attention span for me without indignant objections. Like a tumbled river rock, I had become indecisive and without edges to hold on to. My suppressed anger had fueled an insidious depression that became ever more deeply embedded. I needed to be "seen" and yet I invariably chose the steps to invisibility.

My husband, bewildered and stymied by my depression, a problem that he could neither fix nor solve, nevertheless hung in there with me. When at last I began to deconstruct my life, I spewed out floods of anger and dumped this vitriol on him in a newfound, angry voice, speaking my mind as he had often demanded. Now, like a Chinese wish that was granted, he got more than he had expected. It is a tribute to both of us that we managed to go through this dark stage together and survive to realize that we had completed most of the puzzles and difficulties posed in our complicated and ultimately good marriage.

> **Journal entry, December 27, 1998:** Neil has been reading the new biography by A. Scott Berg of Charles Lindbergh. I found him with tears streaming over some passages he had marked with my initials, MFB. He wanted to read them to me as he wept. "This is the difference between us," he said. The passages were as follows: "He (her therapist) told her (Anne Morrow Lindbergh) that she had every attribute of an artist except one—and that was the conviction that it was more important to cultivate one's own garden than anyone else's." She countered that that was true of most women . . . but he suggested that this was not about gender so much as about her upbringing—that as Anne realized, "I had been made to feel that what I did for others was all that was right but what I did for myself was wrong." Later in comparing her husband to St. Exupéry, whom she loved: the motivation of one was love, understanding, insight, compassion for human beings, she wrote of the Frenchman. "The motivation of the other is conquest—success—achievement."
>
> I attempted to comfort Neil by saying we each had our gifts and that is why we make such a good couple. Yet it was clear he had begun to understand what I was emerging from.

Cornelius Holland Bull III • 1925–2004

In the year 2000, after my depression had lifted permanently, I was able to write about Neil:

> So much of my anger and frustration has been with the scrim of depression lifted now for three and a half years. My feelings are clearer. . . . My ability to see him clearly has sharpened and I am able to be more balanced in my thoughts about him. I am also less fearful of my ability to speak out and say what I feel. It must be easier for him if sometimes uncomfortable. At the same time, I am also full of admiration for his commitment to, and passion for, his projects, and for his great impact on people. Neil is my beloved companion and life mate. Without him life is inconceivable. For forty-six years he kept me on my toes—pushing

me sometimes painfully beyond my limits—but always growth-directed. I have found the limits of my strength and beyond. He is never dull, always fun, irritating, infuriating, stimulating, steadfast, quick to apologize, improve himself. Right wrongs. He has been as passionately and consistently committed and as sometimes misguided a parent as I. He is generous, innovative and consistent in his devotion. It's our differentness that has sparked growth in us both.

✦ ✦ ✦

Journal entry, October 1986: I have been silent to a large extent about Neil in this journal except to exorcise my anger and to try to fight my way clear of his very powerful influence. His presence is so large that one can lose sight of his remarkable qualities. His energy is stupendous; it is really on a heroic scale. What drives that motor is a mystery as it is coupled with humor, enthusiasm, and ingenuity that boggle my mind. I have lived with this steamroller for so long that I really have little idea of how different from most men he is. I know no one else like him.

Our final year together, in the immediacy dictated by his advancing stage-four cancer, gave us the chance to dot the i's and cross the t's as much as was possible in our story. The stage was set for his peaceful death and, in due time, for my vibrant independent life as a finally outspoken widow. These words by Madeleine L'Engle, in *Two-Part Invention*, capture my feeling about our marriage.

Our love has been anything but perfect and anything but static.
Inevitably there have been times when one of us has outrun the

other and has had to wait patiently for the other to catch up. There have been times when we have misunderstood each other, demand- ed too much of each other, been insensitive to the other's needs. I do not believe there is any marriage where this does not happen. The growth of love is not a straight line, but a series of hills and valleys. I suspect that in every good marriage there are times when love seems to be over. Sometimes these desert lines are simply the only way to the next oasis, which is far more lush and beautiful after the desert crossing than it could possibly have been without it.

✦ ✦ ✦

After Neil's death, having been cleared of depression and desirous of ridding myself of the last remaining secrets, I decided to tell my children about my long relationship with Ben. I knew the cor- rosive effects of a legacy of silence and did not want to pass it on to them. Not only were they mature adults in their forties, they all had first-hand experience with therapy and "soul-searching," and I was fairly certain that they would have no trouble either in perceiving the benefits of this secret part of my adult life. I think I told Holly first, but don't remember either the nature of our talk or her reaction.

March 19, 2006, Sheraton Commander: We're in a Cambridge hotel suite, my two sons and I—they sprawled at the foot of a king-sized bed, I propped against the headboard. They are grown men now, but with the resurgent kid quality that overtakes sib- lings together after a lengthy separation. I am rarely alone with them without their families or their sister; this may be the first time in years. It is the first time we've been together since their father's death two years ago. I've just dropped the bombshell on them, and I see the awe and disbelief on these two beloved faces. There was never any secret about my friendship and correspon- dence with Ben, but when I told them about this affair, they were first astonished and then they cheered, both incredulous that the relationship had gone on for thirty-three years. There was a great sense of relief and release for me to make a clean breast of it all. They were both relieved and I think pleased that I'd had that relationship. It was very satisfying that they had grasped and enlarged upon the impact on me of Neil's lack of intimacy—and we also acknowledged what Neil had not had in *his* life. But they also looked at me with a lot of new insight and understanding.

+ + +

I met Ben in person no more than ten times during our three-decade-long connection, and those meetings were never longer than a few hours, time stolen out of busy lives. What would we have been without one another? His patience and generosity of spirit, his willingness to outlast my terrors, his insistence on my worth when I most doubted, and the challenge he invariably urged in the face of my emotional uncertainty buttressed and supported my growth. The integrity, the lucid clarity of his thought and his stature as a human being gave me a sense of worth in the richness of our exchange and in his ongoing interest. His love would carry me across some deep and perilous waters; his patience and the fact that I could trust him fortified my existence. He was one of the few people I felt safe enough to speak to honestly, to disagree with, and to fight with without fear of loss. We never pussy-footed around race, about my Catholic upbringing, about any hot political issues of the times. The intensity and excitement between us never waned. He was nearing ninety when I last saw him, his arms loaded with red roses. We knew it was our last meeting and we gave it the serene benediction and farewell that our remarkable and fortunate communion deserved. We had crossed a great divide together and found home.

+ + +

Interlude: On the evening of August 4, 2005, I attended a performance of Osvaldo Golijov's *Ainadamar,* an opera about Federico Garcia Lorca, at the Santa Fe Opera House. Afterwards, I encountered a group of people gathered around a man who had collapsed in the parking lot. I am a trained Hospice worker, so I joined the others in making him as comfortable as possible. I put my shawl under his head and covered him with my rain jacket. Calls were made to 911 and someone went to get help from the opera staff. He was still lucid and, in a weak voice, was able to answer the questions of a doctor who had been in the audience. As the man was unaccompanied, I sat down next to him and held his hands to give him comfort and the reassurance that he was not alone. It was too much for him to say any more but he held on with a good grip until he began slipping away. He died peacefully before the ambulance arrived. We knew only that his name was Hunter and that he was from Carlsbad, New Mexico. A few days later, I found his obituary in a Santa Fe paper and dissolved into tears when I learned that his full name was Father Alcuin Hunter, and that he had been a Catholic priest.

✛ ✛ ✛

Journal entry, August 13, 1987: My father's birthday. He would have been 80 today. How he would have adored celebrating with lots of friends, lots of feasting, jokes and dancing. There was such vitality and exuberance in him, a rotund, earthy Zorba who led his life at 100 mph. His generous, open-hearted life and above all his fierceness and humor are as alive with me as ever. He was the first of a line of charismatic men in my life. He imprinted me with a taste for vibrant, active, and interesting men of the sort I have been lucky to know well. His rich, quick-witted personality set a standard in a line that extends to the present, especially in his grandsons.

I expect his penchant for indulging in good food and cigarettes contributed to his premature death in 1955. If he had lived two years longer he would have met Neil—his match in energy, humor and charisma—and two years after that, his first grandchild. It is hard to think of these things now in retrospect. I mourn them in a way I could not before. That he and Neil did not meet is something I regret. Though I have learned that it is difficult to have two lions at one's table, in this case, with their shared love of me to unite them, I think they would have gotten on extremely well, each a challenge to the other. It blows my mind to think of those two forces together, sharing the laughter that came so readily and consistently to each.

Me as daughter and wife

✦ ✦ ✦

During the early 1950s, Pate sponsored a brilliant Polish under-
ground fighter, Jerzy Pietron, whom he encouraged to go to Harvard Business School. Jerzy told me much later that Father Hip had
tried to convince him to marry me, thus assuring my future with a
successful man. Jerzy did take me out, took me skiing, and later invited me to accompany him to his Business School Ball, but, being
fifteen years older than me, pleaded with Father that he was too
old to marry me. In retrospect, I think Hip would have been elated with my own choice of husband. And his grandchildren would
have reduced him to utter bondage. He is in my children: his sense
of drama, his singing voice in Neil, his broad chest and capacity to
plunge in and do anything in Sam, and his capacity to counsel, to
listen, and work with people in Holly. In each of them is his sense
of humor, of fun, of delectable outrage.

My father was my guardian—that is what I was instructed to
call him. When I introduced him to others, to my college friends,
for example, I added that he was *my guardian*. It isn't a term one
hears much now, aside from people appointed by courts in cases
where individuals need such assistance. For me, it meant a special
relationship, beyond being one of his parishioners. I envied his altar boys, who served Mass and went with him to Braves and Red
Sox games, but he was not their guardian. Guardian came to mean
to me what "father" signified to others. He was an affectionate, ac-
cessible presence I could always count on and who clearly cared for
me—more than I realized until long after he died. Through my
life I've had a fearless and instinctive certainty of being cared for,
of someone up there watching me and keeping me safe. It often
feels to me that Father Hip, a genius at knowing the right people
and getting things done, is still operating on my behalf.

Journal entry, circa 2010: I have been in Maine with my friends, Peter and Ellie Kuniholm, who have a blueberry farm on the Damariscotta River. It was bought by Ellie's father, Gordon Merriam, after World War II. After retiring from the diplomatic corps, he lived on for fifty years until his death at 99 several years ago. During my visit we sat in the evening by the fireplace, burning wood that Gordon had split, and laid down and read excerpts from his daily record of 1959. Peter often refers now to his father-in-law's daybook as he manages the woods and fields and the river shoreline to see what Gordon was doing about drainage, pruning, or whether to burn the blueberry fields. His books, his papers, his presence—all continue to rustle around the days. How utterly different from mine is Ellie's experience of a father. He was a presence in her life until she was in her late sixties. She has siblings and cousins and friends with whom to reminisce about him. Such immediate intimacy of day-to-day life in a family with one's father was never part of my experience. By the time I knew that Father Hip was my father, he had been dead for thirty years.

It is a blessing that Father Hip was not a tepid backwater but a swift stream who left me with memories of him that remain vivid. But, unlike Ellie, I cannot access his papers or live in his lingering atmosphere, nor relish the affectionate friendship of an adult daughter with her father. I must always cross the barrier of secrecy and project my longing back over the years with an element of the forbidden; I am always nearing the edge of that swift, sparkling river and never able to plunge in.

Mary Gordon's book, *The Shadow Man,* is about her life-long effort to know her father, who died when she was seven. What struck me most was her memory of him saying to her, "I love you more than God." This naked declaration made me reflect on how circumscribed my father must have felt, how constrained this naturally ebullient and passionate man must have been by his lack of freedom to publicly express his pride and love for me. While he must have longed to openly express his affection, he was forced to edit his love and, in so doing, I now realize, he was modeling for me a wariness about committing to a deep relationship. As a result, until much later in life, I found it difficult to say *I love you.* The phrase was fraught with danger; it might not be returned in kind, leaving me feeling vulnerable and foolish. Loving Father as I did, not as my father, but as a family friend, as my parish priest and my guardian, I was bound by many degrees of separation.

If he had lived another twenty-five years, what other secrets might have emerged concerning, say, his under-used talents in the church, or his relationship with my mother? I'd give a great deal to have more time with him and the chance to talk over our shared secret life. I might come to know why my mother revealed my father's identity to others but would never share that information with me, not even with her dying breath. Was it an oath or promise that sealed her lips to me? Her shame? Or some issue with me? I will never know. Would Father have "come out" as my father when I married Neil? Had he lived, he would surely have been the one to marry us.

While speaking of Father Hip with a college friend, whose eyes lit up as she remembered him, I was swept with so fervent a need for his presence, not as a memory but as a loving father I could truly acknowledge and touch, and who would finally recognize me as his daughter. In 1995, the Metropolitan Opera added surtitles to performances and I was finally able to understand the words that accompany the great scene of farewell (*Lebwohl*) in the final act of Wagner's *Die Walküre*. In a scene that always leaves me in tears, an open and passionate declaration of paternal love, the god Wotan, forced by his wife to punish his daughter, Brunhilde, encloses her in a ring of fire and sings:

> *Farewell, you bold, wonderful child! You, my heart's holiest pride.*
> *. . . I must lose you whom I loved—you, laughing joy of my eyes.*

PETERBOROUGH, MARCH 2019

I consider and mull over mother's final years from the perspective of my own. Unlike me, she did not seem really happy at the end of her life. It was difficult to see this objectively at the time. I suspect her general health went into a long, slow decline, altering her humor. I have used the word bitterness, yet that does not seem to fit, is not the exact word; "irritability" might be more accurate. And there was something much deeper. She never experienced the prolonged release I have felt from finally offloading all our secrets.

My home in Peterborough, New Hampshire

Most people at the end of their lives, if they have the chance to reflect, have a version of their own life story that they tell themselves. Having refused to disclose to me so significant a part of her life, i.e. her relationship with Father Hip, she left me no idea what story she told herself, even as I reconstruct my own story. Nor did she receive the comfort of speaking her truth to her husband of over twenty years. He was a loving and devoted partner to her and I feel would have had a compassionate response to what she had lived through, what she had both endured and given up in order to raise me. She could not seem to break the rigid habit of silence that her fear dictated, and yet had she broken out of that bondage, I feel she would have profoundly deepened both my relationship with her and hers with Jack. I'll never know.

I have been blessed with the loving upbringing that she and Father Hip provided for me. While the severe consequences of the secrecy and shame I carried led me unconsciously into depression and suicidal impulses that made up a long, dark side of my life, I was loved and cherished more than enough to give me the strength both to withstand the years of depression and to search for and adjust to my true identity. I was lucky enough to live into this more open and accepting era in which, when I was ready to speak, I could do so without the certain fear of shame and vilification that my parents would have faced. When I was born in the dark, difficult days of the Depression, and in the midst of a deeply bigoted and judgmental time in the Catholic Church, my parents were left with few options. Thank heavens they chose, with courage, the difficult plan to keep me and raise me themselves. This book grew out of a sense of responsibility to a dream of mine to honor them and their parenting of me in the face of all that the Church dictated against their doing so.

I had not read about an experience similar to mine, nor had I ever met another child of a priest until I spoke with Vincent Doyle in Ireland when I was over eighty. I felt a responsibility to telling this story that also fulfills my wish to set the story straight for my family. My own children, who have lived through its unfolding, still find its facts and sequences confusing.

This story's written evolution from my early letters, the journals I started keeping when I learned the identity of my father, through my graduate work, and then this memoir, has given me the chance to reexamine my life, and that of Florence and Father Hip, as my parents and as a couple, and to give me a broad overview of what has been a rocky but romantic and eventful road that I've traveled to get here—shedding baggage along the way to travel as experienced travelers do, lightly.

In my early eighties I fell unexpectedly and deeply in love. I was no longer hampered by a lifelong habit of holding back in fear of being hurt; I encountered no guilt, no barriers to being totally open both to being loved and to fully returning that love. It was the highlight of this stage of my life. Free of the burden that binding secrecy had imposed on me, I could at last experience a full relationship. I lost my beloved Sandy too soon, though in the process received further acceptance by his children, who welcomed me into their circle to care for him in his final illness and mourn with them his death. In so doing they helped ease my lifelong issues around funerals, where I had either been unacknowledged or my presence had made the family uncomfortable. Their kindness made me a legitimate family member as they grieved and cared for their father.

The grace of my love affair would not have been possible without the long road that preceded it. A seasoned widow of fourteen years, I was totally at peace with my life. That tranquility brought my dear friend to me with his openness, honesty, and profound sense of himself. He allowed me to be at home on this new ground.

My husband had supported me in my long search for clarity, suffered through my emergence, and urged me to write to the point that, in his final week, he struggled to his feet, put his hands on my shoulders to steady himself, and hoarsely demanded, "Speak, speak, speak!" He and my children felt the impact of my difficult legacy as a child of a priest; they were, like me, unwitting victims of the fallout from an outworn and untenable policy of binding celibacy for its clergy. Only recently, after the nine hundred years of required celibacy in the church, has there been a secret set of guidelines to deal with priests' children.

Mine is only one version of what is an all too common and until now darkly concealed story in the Church. I was more fortunate than most priests' children. My father was committed to my well-being and to being an ongoing part of my life. Others have been met with a range of austere rejection and brutal denial. All of us have had to deal with the poisonous silence around our true identity. Having spent a long stretch of my life clearing the burdensome mysteries of my story, I urge the Catholic Church to make an open policy that will enable children of priests to know our father, our origins, and the truth of who we are without the debilitating shame and secrecy that its current clandestine policy engenders.

I hold close a dream: I am with my mother and father as an adult, and we all know the truths of our family. We gaze deeply and lovingly into one another's eyes, and I take them in my arms to hug them close. I thank them. I express the hope that I have fulfilled all the brave dreams they had for me.

POSTSCRIPT

The following is the first draft of the letter to the Pope. I sent it to Vincent Doyle and he used it as is. When friends asked if I had a response, I was told by Vincent that, "He [the Pope] was as likely to drop in one afternoon for a cup of tea."

September 2017

Your Holiness:

I feel fortunate to have lived to see your election to the Papacy. The promise of needed change that we had longed for and was begun with Pope John XXIII is at last again under way.

Like Your Holiness, I have grown older through the great changes in the world of the last eighty years. I was born in 1936 into the matrix of the predominantly Irish Boston Catholic Diocese presided over by Cardinal Richard O'Connell. With his Victorian, straight-laced mindset he ruled his diocese with a tight fist. My mother was a young single woman, and my father, the pastor of a tiny Polish parish at the edge of a mill town fifteen miles from Boston. With her mother's help, my parents chose the profound risk of raising me in an era when exposure in that repressed atmosphere would have been catastrophic for them both. As a cover story, I was put into foster care for a year until my grandmother could "adopt" me.

My father secretly cared for us until his early death at forty-eight, when I was eighteen and a freshman in college. I didn't know him as other than my parish priest, and my "guardian." I saw a lot of him and loved him like a genial but necessarily separate father figure and family friend.

Mine was a loving, good childhood. Yet the impact from the secrecy of my situation was very long and taxing. My mother did not tell me she was my real mother until I was thirty-five and had three nearly grown children of my own. She refused to tell me the identity of my father. Not until thirteen years later, at her death, did I learn the identity of my father. Thus, at forty-eight, with the facts finally at hand, I could begin to integrate this new story into my sense of my identity, my marriage, my children, and begin to heal my long, intermittent, puzzling, and suicidal depression. It was nearly impossible for professional psychotherapists to wrap their heads around my experience; I was like a tree strangled with lianas, distorting, and stifling me.

Until this, my eighty-first year, I had never spoken with another priest's child. I had tried to find others—like an orphan looking for one's lost tribe. Just as the secrecy deprived me of feeling a part of either my mother or father's family, I was "adopted" after all, so the secrecy and shame has kept priests' children from the comfort and support of knowing one another.

The Church, always cowardly in the face of scandal, hid and swept us all under the rug to save its reputation. It never considered the human fallout from its failure to acknowledge us, the blameless children, much less offer compassion for our plight. Not only did it render us invisible, but it made it impossible for us to have the recognition we so needed from our fathers. I was strong enough, and grounded in loving parents, to fight my way to serenity and mental stability. Many others are not as fortunate.

It is imperative that the church immediately (not in fifty to a hundred years) make policy around this serious, chronic, poisonous problem. My simple suggestion is to allow lay/parish priests to marry and let those who wish to practice celibacy as their spiritual practice do so either as parish nuns/priests or monastics. My father was a beloved and remarkable parish priest—unsuited to celibacy but eminently suited to serving his parishioners in a wise, compassionate manner.

Until I was nearly fifty, I did not know and could not claim my own mother and father as "my parents." Only after their deaths did I appreciate that they took full responsibility for their "sin" and raised me at great risk and personal sacrifice, that they were strong enough for the emotional confusion and strain that such potent secrecy imposes on human beings.

I pray that you will have the strength and wisdom to change the vow of celibacy for lay priests, and lead the church to care for this army of bewildered illegitimate children who suffer the stigma and consequences of their birth.

With urgency and deep respect,

Mimi Bull

ACKNOWLEDGMENTS

I HAVE BEEN FORTUNATE to have a loyal band of family, friends, and professionals to encourage and support me to the completion of this story. My profound appreciation is due to the following:

To my children, Neil, Sam, and Holly Bull, who have loved and prodded and believed me in my need to tell this story.

To my four granddaughters, Maia Bull, Samantha Krieg King, Calli Rose Bull, and Lia Bull-Krieg, and great-granddaughter Amara King, for whom I started this project so that they might later make some sense of an unusual and complicated part of their heritage.

To my son Neil, who in these recent years of living with me has made this project possible in the thousands of thoughtful ways he lightens my load, not the least in his ever witty and delightful company. He has been midwife to the completion of this memoir—without him, it would be just another work in progress.

To Louisa Sarofim, whose long friendship and kindness have given me an annual summer setting in Santa Fe to recharge the writing muse in the sublime beauty and renewal of its atmosphere.

To Connie Goodman, for her steady, laughter-filled friendship and the long-ago nudge she gave me to apply to work for George Kennan.

To my friend Charles Reinhart, who has prodded me to speak, believed in me, and cheered my progress with this project.

To Kate Gleason, poet extraordinaire, under whose encouraging wings this book grew. And to my fellow writers in her weekly workshops who listened and queried and cheered me on.

To Tina Rapp, for her wise counsel, her encouragement, and her friendship.

To Peggy Cappy, for keeping me on my feet, breathing and moving for the last two decades.

To Marieve Rugo, friend and staunch fellow writer for modeling persistence with her own riveting memoir.

To Mike Rezendes, whose articles in the *Boston Globe* opened a whole new stage in the story, and who introduced me to Coping International, where, after a long life, I recently met others dealing with the fallout of their lives as priests' children.

To Jane Eklund, my editor, who "grokked" this story and firmly and unobtrusively prodded me to make it better. She took my story and turned it into a book. To Sarah Bauhan, who believed in publishing it, and to Henry James, whose design enhances the story.

To a beloved recent presence in my life, the late Sandy Isaacs, who nourished me through the last months with his singular brand of TLC.

To the special town of Peterborough, New Hampshire, and my friends here in the Monadnock Region who have given me a supportive matrix from which to sally forth and a welcoming return—always.

And in loving gratitude to my late husband, Cornelius Bull—Neil—who stayed the forty-seven-year course with me and raised with me three great children. He endured and supported me through all the roughest stages of this story and provided consistent surprise and adventure from the first minute I saw him.

And, finally, in memory of and in loving appreciation of my parents, Father Hip and Florence, who prepared me so well for the very full life I was to lead. I continue to be astonished at the courage with which they undertook to raise me. The long process of writing this book gave me time to think of and better understand them both as a couple and as my parents. If they were alive today, I hope they would accept my revelation of their secret that for so long they had to keep.

Father Hip on a trip to Florida when I was 13 years old—the only trip I went on with both my mother and father, 1949